Merry Chris
Patrick 😊
—Kym

MORE DEVILS THAN HELL
CAN HOLD

STORIES BY
MORGAN BOYD

Patriak

Ryan,

Hope you see

the world!

More Devils Than Hell Can Hold

Cover Design: Eric Beetner

First Printing 2021

ISBN: 978-1-7372338-0-0

TABLE OF CONTENTS

For Moe & Rivs

MORE DEVILS THAN HELL CAN HOLD

STORIES BY
MORGAN BOYD

A Hell of a Hideout

As the sun sank into the darkness, headlights appeared on the horizon. A pick-up truck with an empty chicken coop in the back pulled to the side of the road. Putting away my thumb, I climbed into the cab. An old woman sat behind the wheel, and a diapered chimpanzee sat bitch.

"Name's Henrietta Pule," she said under the dome light. "This here's Marvin."

"Howard Jones."

"Where you heading?"

"Next town over."

"Pottsville, eh? You look nervous."

"Monkeys have that effect on me."

"Don't worry about Marvin," she said, pulling back onto the road. "He's harmless as a child. Don't mean to be rude neither, but Marvin ain't no monkey. He's an ape. There's a difference. Monkeys' smaller, and apes got no tail."

Marvin grunted, and smacked the old woman in the face.

"Ouch, dang it, Marvin. Be gentle with mama."

The sun died, and the night cast shadows on my travel companions. Marvin's silhouette loomed as the headlight's residuals illuminated Henrietta's lined face. Every so often, she took her eyes off the road and glanced at me.

"What's a fine looking fellow like yourself want with an ugly town like Pottsville?"

"Work."

"Notice the quail coop in the back?"

"Thought it chicken."

"I can see how you might think that, but the coop's for quail. My husband and I, God rest his soul, raised bird twenty years. Troy's dead now a decade, but me and the quail is still going strong. I'm in need of help, and you look like a hard worker. What do you say? Pays a decent wage, and you get three square meals a day. Marvin stop. Mama's trying to drive."

Marvin smacked the old lady on the head, and the truck swerved over the yellow line. Fortunately, no vehicle approached from the opposite direction through the enveloping fog.

"I appreciate the offer, but I'm no aviary expert."

"Ain't hard. Just tending a little bird. You'll be fine."

Any semblance of direction disappeared in the fog as we turned onto a dirt road. After a considerable amount of time spent bouncing along potholes, we stopped at a rusty barbed wire gate. Henrietta opened the driver's side door, and Marvin bounded from the vehicle. Knuckling to the gate, he flung it open, and disappeared into the misty night.

"Get back here," Henrietta yelled. "Sometimes that chimp really runs a gal down. Mind closing the gate after I pull through?"

The thought of walking into the dark unknown with a savage beast on the loose sent my heart racing. Quickly, I hopped out, closed the gate, and hopped back into the cab.

"Marvin don't always act this way. He's normally civilized. Dresses and bathes himself, drinks from a wine glass, and uses the toilet, well sometimes. He ain't so good on trips. That's why he's diapered," the old lady said, parking the truck.

"Wait here while I find that silly chimp, and get him inside the ranch house."

As the old woman disappeared into the fog, a pungent odor filled my nostrils. I figured Marvin had left a surprise for me in the cab, but then I remembered the diaper. The fetor drove me from the cab into the brume, but once outside, the stench intensified.

Henrietta returned to the truck, carrying a lantern in one hand, and holding the side of her face with the other.

"Sorry to keep you waiting. Follow me, and I'll show you your quarters. I suspect that look on your face has something to do with the smell."

"What is it?"

"Quail dung. You'll get used to it. Some of the hands I've hired in the past acted like they'd never been on a ranch before when they got a whiff of the place. Bunch of complainers, but not Johnny. He never grumbled. Thirty years of bird shit don't smell of roses. My husband dug a pond behind the barn, but we didn't fill it with water. Even built a dock, so you can dump the manure out in the middle. Named it Tahoe. Troy always got a kick out of that. Johnny never saw the humor in it, but I don't think he got the joke."

We passed the barn, walking along Tahoe's shore until we arrived at a two-wheel camper trailer that hitched to a flea. Henrietta unlocked the door, and shone the lantern inside. Cockroaches scurried for cover.

"Now you're lakeside," Henrietta said. "This is where Johnny stayed. He was my best worker to date. I've had more duds quit on me than I can count. You don't seem like one of those good-for-nothings. You have an honest face. Tomorrow, you get the grand tour."

Henrietta shut the door, leaving me in darkness. I plopped down on the lumpy box spring, pulled a crusty wool blanket over my body, and fell asleep. I dreamt I was rowing a sinking boat in a lake of shit. The harder I paddled, the faster the boat foundered until the feces flooded the small vessel. I tried swimming through the excrement, but the more I struggled, the more engulfed I became until only my head remained above the scat, and a great many cockroaches and flies blackened my countenance.

I hopped out of bed in a cold sweat, shivering and swatting at my face. To my horror, the droning flies did not dissipate upon waking, but instead intensified. Flinging open the door, I stumbled outside as the rising sun burned the morning fog.

The old lady wasn't kidding about the shit pond. It looked about fifty-by-thirty feet in diameter, and a rickety wooden pier led from the shore to the middle of the manure. At the end of the pier, an old rusty wheelbarrow lay on its side.

I walked over to the barn.

"What 'cha doing?" Henrietta said behind me.

"Nothing," I sputtered, spinning around to find the old lady pointing a shotgun at me.

Her left eye black and swollen shut.

"Said I'd give you the grand tour," she said. "Why so jumpy?"

"Guns make me nervous."

"Oh, this old thing," Henrietta said. "Think I'd shoot you? That's a laugh. I wish Troy were here to hear that one. There's an old fox digging under my barn, nabbing my bird. He's a crafty Reynard, but when I get his vulpine butt in my crosshairs, I'll light him up brighter than Aurora Borealis. Over the years, I've shot darn near

4

every known predator in these parts. Opossums, raccoons, snakes, hawks, rats, coyotes, and once I even got a bobcat. I shoot 'em, and stuff 'em. Troy did a little taxidermy on the side, and I just sort of kept up the tradition. Got a zoo of stuffed and mounted animals inside the ranch house, and I'm looking to add Mr. Fox to my fold. Bet you're hungry."

Henrietta led me to the ranch house, and made me wait in the front yard while she went inside. The fear of Marvin mauling me returned. He must have really socked it to the old lady. Not that I blamed him. That damned ape should be swinging from trees in Africa, not diapered somewhere in central California. Not to mention, Henrietta seemed like the type who might elicit a thrashing now and again on account of her continuous blabbering. Twenty-four hours had yet to pass in her presence, and I was already sick of the old bag.

"Hope you like beans 'cause I got a whole mess of 'em," she said returning with an open can.

When I finished the lukewarm legumes, Henrietta gave me the grand tour. The property consisted of a series of rocky gray hummocks, a junkyard of rusty old cars, and various refuse. The ranch house, the barn and the shit pond occupied the only level ground on the property.

"Bet you're rearing to have a look at them bird," Henrietta said after we walked the perimeter of barbwire fence.

The old lady unlocked and opened the barn door. As the light crept across the dirt floor, a multitude of cockroaches scurried for cover under the rows and stacks of cooped quail. We entered, and a new concentrated stench wobbled me.

"Waste trays need changing every day or the roaches eat the dung. Fill the wheelbarrow with the scat, and dump it off the pier. Fill the troughs with water, and the feeders with corn twice a day. When a quail lays an egg, remove it before the bird eats it. Well, what are you waiting for? You're already a can of beans behind. Oh, and one more thing. If I catch you stealing any of my bird or egg, I'll have Sheriff Braden whirling around you so quick, you'll think he was a cyclone. He's a personal friend of mine, so don't think I'm shooting cold water. I don't mean to threaten. Just something I got to say. We clear?"

"As a lake," I said, and Henrietta left me to my chores.

The trays brimmed with bird droppings, so I filled the wheelbarrow, and dumped the dung off the pier. The burlap feedbags were fifty pounders, so I was puzzled as to how the old lady could tote such massive sacks by her lonesome.

Over the next three days, I acclimated to the putrescent smell, but my appetite didn't acclimate to the food. Three days of lukewarm beans were three days too many. On the fourth day, I pinched a few quail egg, and ate them raw, hiding the shells under my mattress in the trailer.

"You're doing a fine job," Henrietta said, handing me a half a can of beans for breakfast. "I ain't seen this place so clean since Johnny had your job. How'd you like to join me in the ranch house tonight to listen to the World Series?"

"I'd like that."

At sundown, I knocked on the ranch house's withered front door, but there was no answer, so I knocked again. The door vibrated, and I heard the unmistakable call of the wild.

"Marvin, no," Henrietta yelled as the door swung open, and I found myself inches from an angry chimp wearing a silk robe. Marvin curled his upper lip, giving me a face-to-face view of his yellow choppers.

Henrietta smacked the ape on the back of the head with the butt of a firearm, but Marvin brushed it off like an annoying fly. He let out an ear-shattering scream, and lunged at me, but fell short, snoring loudly on the ground by my feet. Henrietta stood behind Marvin with a funny looking rifle.

"Marvin gets surly about visitors. Mind carrying him to his room?"

I bent down, and noticed the tranquilizer dart in the ape's hairy neck. Waving my hand in front of the chimp, I made certain he was really unconscious.

"Don't worry. He ain't waking after that dose," Henrietta said, and pulled the dart from his neck.

Apprehensively, I lifted Marvin into my arms, and carried him into the ranch house.

The living room was crowded with stuffed and mounted animals. Henrietta wasn't lying about having shot every predator known to quail in these parts. Preserved hawks hung from the ceiling in various attack positions. On shelves surrounding each wall, a multitude of vehement and petrified opossums, raccoons, skunks, coyotes, and even a bobcat sat ready to pounce.

The dining room table was set for two, complete with candles, a bottle of wine, and steak and potatoes. I figured dinner was for me, but the candles were half-burnt, the wine bottle empty, and the meat mostly eaten. Henrietta led me down a hallway into a bedroom.

"This is Marvin's room."

I placed the sleeping ape on the bed, taking in the spectacle. A spoiled sixteen-year-old girl didn't have it so good. The walls were pink and lined with glass display cabinets. Inside each cabinet stood rows of large children's dolls.

"There you go my little angel," Henrietta said, tucking the ape under the lacy pink covers. "Mama's sorry she had to put you to sleep with the dart gun, but you were misbehaving, and mama hates misbehaving."

She gave him a goodnight kiss, and turned off the bedroom light before we returned to the dining room.

"Have a seat in the living room while I clean up Marvin's dinner," Henrietta said.

Henrietta took away the plates with the mostly eaten steaks. Later, I planned to sneak around back, and find that meat in the garbage.

Henrietta brought me a can of warm beans when she finished in the kitchen, and turned on an enormous old clunker of a radio. Several stuffed quail perched on top of the ancient refrigerator sized apparatus. For a few minutes, the old bag adjusted the large black dials until men announcing baseball became audible above crackling static.

When the game ended, Henrietta bade me goodnight, and showed me to the door. Outside it was pitch black and foggy. Hunger led me to the slop barrel behind the ranch house. I rummaged through the refuse until a low moan, emanating from the ground, drew my attention away from my quest for beef scraps.

Light peeked out a crack in a bomb shelter door, leading down to the ranch house's basement. I peered through the sliver of light, but averted my eyes, and fled to my trailer at the sight of a naked man standing over Henrietta.

Early the next morning, I gathered the eggshells under my mattress, and walked to the end of the pier. Leaning over the side, I dug a hole in the shit with my hands. When the aperture was deep enough, I discarded the remnants of my snaffled meal. Gaining my feet, I stepped wrong, and spilled off the pier.

The dung acted like quicksand. Each movement caused me to sink deeper. Eventually I was able to grasp the wooden pier. After a good deal of wiggling and rocking back and forth, I broke free from the crud, and hoisted myself out of the shit, but my left boot remained ensconced in the crap.

Leaning over the pier on my knees, I looked into the imprint my body made in the shit pit. Holding a pylon with my left hand, I reached into the closing turd hole, and seized my boot, but I was unable to dislodge the footwear. I groped around the boot's toe until I felt a long solid object partially obstructing my boot's freedom. It felt like a wooden dowel or a metal rod. I worked the front of the boot back and forth until it came lose along with the object blocking it: a long decaying bone.

I was using the hose on the side of the barn to clean up when I heard the sound of an approaching vehicle. I peered around the corner, and saw a sheriff's truck coming up the drive.

Hiding in the barn, I peeked through the cracked door. A heavyset man wearing a white cowboy hat exited the truck, and approached Henrietta on the porch. My heart raced when they stared at the barn. Eventually, the sheriff tipped his hat, climbed into his truck, and drove away.

I was wheeling quail apples out of the barn when Henrietta rounded the corner. She had the tranquilizer rifle in one hand and Marvin's hand in the other.

"Sheriff Braden stopped by this morning," Henrietta said. "Said a convict recently escaped from the penitentiary a few counties over. Fellow in the wanted poster was you. Wanted dead or alive."

I noticed Henrietta wasn't holding the tranquilizer gun, but rather the shotgun.

"Figured I'd let your whereabouts slide on account of the fine job you're doing 'round here, but then Marvin brought something to my attention. Go on Marvin, what'd you find in Tahoe?"

Marvin opened his clenched fist, revealing eggshells.

"Know what we do with thieves on Pule Ranch? Marvin, no. Let mama alone. Marvin stop."

Marvin walloped the old lady in the shoulder, and I took off running, but a blast of buckshot knocked me to the ground. Henrietta raised the shotgun to fire again, but Marvin grabbed the gun barrel.

"No, Marvin. Let mama have it," Henrietta demanded as I staggered to my feet.

The old woman and the ape struggled for control of the shotgun until it discharged, and half of Henrietta's face disappeared. The chimp looked at the weapon in his hands, and then at Henrietta's brains oozing from the side of her head. Throwing the gun against the barn, he shook the old lady. When she didn't rouse, he let out a guttural bellow, and looked at me with yellow eyes and malcontent. I was a goner for sure until a string of words came fast and sharp into my ear from behind.

"Show me your hands," Sheriff Braden demanded.

"Yes, sir," I obliged, bleeding on the ground.

Marvin let out another primordial bellow, and disappeared into the fog.

Sheriff Braden cuffed me, and radioed for backup. Wasn't long before I was all patched up, and back in a cell, but prison didn't seem so bad anymore. Three square meals a day: big meals, but I don't eat the beans. I push them aside. Prisoners keep the floors clean too. Cockroaches don't do well in prison. I've also become somewhat of a celebrity in the hole. Not just because I escaped and lived on the lamb for several weeks. The reason for my brush with fame was solely due to Henrietta Pule.

After Sheriff Braden arrested me, his men searched the property, and found more than just a quail farm. Down in the basement, deputies found a stuffed man, fully erect. It didn't take too long to figure out his identity: Jonathan Brown: a local drifter who'd been missing several months.

After deputies found the preserved corpse, they tore Pule Ranch apart. When they took a backhoe to Tahoe and unearthed a mass grave of human bones, the media literally swarmed like flies on the shit pond. It didn't take long before investigators determined that Henrietta was luring old war vets out to her ranch, stealing their pensions, and burying their bodies under the dung. Old bank records from the victims and bottles of poison found in the back drawer of her vanity confirmed this theory.

The papers picked up on the fact that if I hadn't escaped from prison, and hadn't hid at Pule ranch, Henrietta's crimes might never have been discovered. I've given dozens of interviews to news outlets wanting my side of the story. Some were even national. The other prisoners and even the guards treat me a shade above reproach these days. I sleep pretty well most nights. There is that rare occasion though, when I wake in a cold sweat of terror from a dream of drowning in a shit pond, surrounded by dense fog as Marvin's piercing scream reverberates in my ear.

Arson on the Eastside

I couldn't rouse Big Dave as the fire spread through the living room. He had been up for days smoking crystal and drinking cheap beer before falling asleep. I yelled and punched him, but he remained unconscious as the flames leapt around us.

Nate and my girlfriend Tiffany had safely exited the burning house. Tiffany screamed from the front lawn for us to get out. I tried dragging Big Dave, but he was too heavy. The smoke was thick and the heat unbearable. Begrudgingly, I left my friend and roommate, and crawled on my hands and knees out the front door as a wall exploded behind me into red cinders. In the distance, sirens approached.

Nate, Big Dave, Tiffany, and I rented the three-bedroom house near Portola Drive on the Eastside. Our friends called it the Bro-Hive because we partied there night and day. When we weren't partying, we were surfing Pleasure Point.

Big Dave was an enforcer, controlling the peak at Sewer's. He'd dunk or chase off anybody that dropped in on us, so we always got the best waves. Nate and I were sponsored and destined for the pro-circuit. Tiffany worked at a nearby retail shop, selling over-priced t-shirts and sunglasses to tourists. She had long blonde hair, blue eyes, a little button nose and just the right amount of curves in all the right places. During bikini season, I felt like the luckiest man alive.

Tiffany told the firefighters Big Dave was still inside. They suited up and made their way into the burning Bro-Hive. After several tense moments, two firefighters appeared through the smoke, carrying Big Dave. We stood over our friend to see if he was okay, but he wasn't okay. Big Dave had burned to death.

"Ryan did this," Nate said as I coughed and hugged Tiffany. "He's as good as dead."

We'd been friends with Ryan since middle school. We grew up together surfing the Eastside. Ryan was one of the boys in our pack, and we spent countless nights knocking back beers and burning green bowls with him. The trouble started when Ryan's parents bought him a jacked-up four-runner for his eighteenth birthday.

He pulled up to the Bro-Hive in his new ride. Nate and I hopped in with a twenty-four pack of beer, and we headed to Hollister Hills for an off-road session. Ryan did some donuts, and then he gunned the engine, launching from a huge dirt mound. He hit the jump off-center, and less than twenty-four hours after his parents bought him the truck, Ryan rolled it. Nate wasn't wearing a seatbelt, and was thrown from the vehicle. The truck narrowly missed crushing his scull by a few inches, but his right arm wasn't so lucky. I also wasn't wearing a seatbelt, and broke my back. Ryan was strapped in, and didn't get a scratch.

Rehabilitation took almost a year. When I finally paddled into the lineup again, my skills had diminished. I couldn't snap off the lip or punt for big air anymore. Nate never regained full mobility in his damaged arm, and our surfing dreams evaporated faster than saltwater.

The firefighters doused the inferno, contained the destruction, and halted the threat of the flames advancing toward the neighbors' homes. When the blaze was extinguished, the Bro-Hive was gone. Like Big Dave, only the charred frame of what once was remained.

The police and arson investigators interrogated us for several hours, but it was all a blur. I was grieving the loss of Big Dave, and coming down from meth. I wanted to forget everything and sleep for a week. When the authorities finally let us go, we walked to Nate's mom's place. She lived in the trailer park behind the 7-Eleven on the Eastside. She bought us several frozen pizzas for dinner, and went to bed. I wanted to crash too, but instead we stayed awake, smoking crystal.

We weren't always meth-heads. I never touched the stuff before breaking my back. Ryan introduced us to the drug. I can't speak for Nate, but a profound depression rattled me to the core while rehabilitating. We lost our sponsors, and the lack of physical exertion drove me crazy. The meth got me through those low points. Before long, Big Dave and Tiffany were also smoking, and we began selling for Ryan to supplement our income.

The fallout with Ryan had escalated over money. Ryan owed Nate for a surfboard, but Ryan snapped the board during his first session in the water, and refused to pay. Nate and Big Dave went to Ryan's mom's garage where Ryan lived, and demanded money. When Ryan refused, Big Dave knocked him out. They went through Ryan's belongings, and took his cash and crystal. After their confrontation, Ryan said he'd kill Nate and Big Dave. Nate wasn't taking the threat seriously, but he was laying low.

We stayed up all night at Nate's mom's, smoking meth. At dawn, Nate pulled out the hide-a-bed in the couch. I didn't like the idea of Tiffany lying next to Nate. At one point, I dozed off, and when I woke, I suspected they were groping under the blanket. Nate's mom left us a box of donuts before she went to work. I nibbled at an apple fritter, but after smoking more meth, I lost my appetite. Nate went into his mom's room, and returned with a .38.

"Let's find that fucker," he said. "There's a swell in the water. I bet Ryan's at the Point."

"What are you doing?" Tiffany asked.

"Payback for Big Dave," Nate said.

"But you'll go to jail."

"It's him or me."

"Severn, please talk some sense into him," Tiffany pleaded.

"What is there to say?" Nate asked. "Dave was your boy too. You just going to sit there and let Ryan punk us?"

"We should think about this," I said. "Before doing something stupid."

"I'm taking my mom's beach cruiser to Pleasure Point," Nate said. "You can either get out, or use my sister's mountain bike, and come with."

Tiffany should have taken the pink mountain bike, and Nate should have given me a pump on the cruiser's handlebars, but instead, Nate boosted Tiffany, and I rode the pink mountain bike. We pedaled to Pleasure Point. The tide was low, and the swell was up. An offshore wind hollowed out the curls, making for ideal conditions. Sewer's Peak was beyond crowded. Back in the day, Big Dave would have managed the herd, and we'd have feasted on the best waves.

"See him anywhere?" Nate asked.

"Nope," I said. "Maybe he's surfing the Westside."

"I'm not rolling over there," Nate said. "He'll show up eventually."

Tommy approached us, and said he was sorry to hear about Big Dave. Nate wouldn't talk to him because Tommy was Ryan's boy. I asked him if he'd seen Ryan around, and he said he hadn't, but there was something in his response that made me think he was lying.

"Come on guys," Tiffany said. "I'm getting cold, and I have to go to work. Do you think I can borrow some of your mom's clothes, Nate?"

"I don't see why not."

We pedaled back to Nate's mom's trailer. Nate went into the bathroom, and didn't come out for a longtime. When he finally reappeared, Tiffany exchanged a glance with him, and also disappeared into the bathroom.

After Tiffany left for work, I called my mom. She heard about the fire and Big Dave, and was concerned because she hadn't been able to reach me. I asked her if I could visit. She seemed hesitant, but said Scott would pick me up in front of the 7-Eleven in half-an-hour.

"New ride, huh?" I said as my stepfather pulled alongside me in a cherry red BMW.

"Don't slam the door," he said when I entered. "We saw the fire on the news. I hope you don't think you're moving back in with us."

We didn't talk much on the drive. It was no secret Scott and I didn't get along. He thought I was a lazy bum, living off my mom's money, and I thought the same thing about him. Scott was an alcoholic. He had one of those veiny red noses old people acquire after years of drinking. I never understood what my mom saw in Scott. As we drove through the Capitola Village, I thought about the falling out with my mom.

I had bought a new surfboard with the money I saved working as a security guard at the Boardwalk. The next day, Scott took my new surfboard out of the garage, and left it on the lawn overnight. In the morning, it was gone. I was furious, and demanded he buy me another board, but Scott laughed in my face, so I took my skateboard, and smashed out the windshield and headlights of his truck. He had a conniption, and we came to blows. It was the last straw for my mother, and she booted me. I hadn't been back since.

Scott parked in front of the two-story house my grandfather bought fifty years ago. The house sat on the edge of a bluff over Soquel Creek. Before my mom married Scott, she told me that someday the house would be mine. Scott had other designs. He didn't want her to leave the place to me, and was constantly pressuring her to sell.

I went straight to the refrigerator, and opened one of Scott's Sierra Nevada. I didn't see my mom anywhere inside, so I went out back, and found her working in the garden. She gave me a suspicious look, and then she took off her gloves, and gave me a hug.

"Sorry to hear about your friend," she said. "How are you doing?"

"Still in shock," I said. "Fortunately, I have a great girl helping me through."

"Why didn't she join us?" My mom asked.

"She's working."

"Is there anything I can do to help? What do you think of Scott's new car?"

"I'm all right," I said.

"I know you don't want to hear this right now," she said. "But Scott and I have decided to sell. We found a nice ranch out in Corralitos, and with the extra money we can retire."

"But you said grandpa's house would be mine someday."

"I know, but plans change," she said with a hurt look in her eye.

"This is bullshit," I said. "What about me?"

"I can help you out with school."

Scott sat on the couch, watching a local news channel as I stormed into the house.

"Don't slam the door," he said.

"This beer tastes like shit," I said, and hurled the bottle at his head.

He ducked, and it shattered against the wall.

"Get the fuck out," he said, standing up.

I slammed the front door as hard as I could, and walked back to the Eastside in a rage, snapping parked car's antennas along the way. When I arrived at Nate's mom's trailer, Nate and Tiffany sat side-by-side, but they moved apart as I entered.

"Ever heard of knocking?" Nate asked.

"What's wrong?" Tiffany asked.

"I thought you were working," I said.

"They felt bad, and sent me home," she said.

I told her my mom was selling the house. Tiffany tried to console me, but the more I thought about it, the angrier I became. We smoked meth, and Nate said he had something that would cheer me up. He took a smart phone out of his pocket, and turned it on.

"Do you remember this?" He asked.

"Your old phone," I said.

"Yup," he said. "The one I got before my iPhone."

"So?"

"So don't you remember?" He said, and turned it on.

He found a video, and hit play on the screen. I watched the scene unfold on the tiny monitor. Several years ago, when we were still friends with Ryan, we had beef with a Westsider named Jerry Fields and his buddies. They thought they could surf wherever they pleased and tried to muscle in on our peak, so Big Dave sent them packing. After the incident, Ryan discovered 'Westside' spray-painted across the windshield of his mom's car. Later that night, Ryan bought a gallon of gas, and we rolled up to Jerry's parents' house. Jerry's

18

green Cadillac convertible was parked at the curb. Nate took out his phone and started filming as Ryan doused the Cadillac's interior with gasoline.

"Adios motherfucker," Ryan said to the camera, striking a match, and throwing it over his shoulder into the Cadillac.

The image on the phone went completely white as the fireball exploded.

"Whoops," Nate said when the video ended. "I accidently sent this incriminating evidence to the police."

Tiffany was scared that Ryan would retaliate, but Nate assured her that the best defense was a proactive offense. He said Ryan's hands would be full explaining the video to the police, and that if he went to jail, that meant he wasn't on the street trying to kill us. Tiffany wasn't buying it, but there was no arguing with Nate, so she dropped the subject.

Tiffany's father was on a business trip for a few days, so we stayed at his apartment near downtown. This worked in our favor because Nate's mom was growing weary of us. Nate scored twelve hits of acid from a UCSC student, and bought a twenty-four pack of beer. After we each dropped two hits, the walls in Tiffany's dad's living room rippled in an imaginary breeze as we plowed through the beer.

Nate gave me twenty bucks, and told me to buy another twenty-four pack. I didn't want to leave the apartment, but after several hits of meth, I felt up to the challenge. I borrowed Tiffany's dad's beach cruiser and set out for the liquor store. As I pedaled onto the street, a Honda Civic sideswiped me. I went down on my head, and when I got up off the asphalt, I felt half-flattened. Blood dripped down my face. The Honda pulled over, and a young woman exited from the driver's side.

"Oh my god," she said. "I'm so sorry. I didn't see you. It's like you appeared out of nowhere. Are you okay?"

"I think so," I said. "The bike seems okay too."

"Thank god," she said. "Here, take this."

She handed me two twenty-dollar bills, apologized again, got in her car and drove off into the twinkling haze. I climbed onto the bike, and continued to my destination. When I arrived at the liquor store, I felt fuzzy. I grabbed a twenty-four pack of beer, and stood in line.

"What happened to you?" Tommy said, tapping me on the shoulder, as I was about to pay.

"This chick hit me with her car," I said. "She gave me forty bucks."

"No way," Tommy said. "What are you all about?"

"Nothing," I said. "Just dosing over at Tiff's dad's place."

"For real?"

"Yeah," I said, and paid. "See you around."

Holding the case of beer with one hand in my lap, I held the handlebars with my other hand, and pedaled to the apartment.

"What happened?" Nate asked, popping a beer.

"Are you okay?" Tiffany asked.

"I'm already tired of telling it, but some chick hit me with her car. She felt bad, and gave me forty bucks."

"Who else did you tell?" Nate asked.

"I ran into Tommy at the store."

"What did you say?" Nate asked.

"That we're tripping at Tiffany's dad's apartment."

"Jesus, Severn," Tiffany said. "He's been here before."

"What the fuck," Nate said. "You know he's Ryan's boy."

"I didn't think it was a big deal," I said as Nate grabbed the .38 out of his backpack.

We spent the night chugging beer, and arguing about what to do. Nate paced the floor paranoid that Ryan would find us. At sunrise, the acid was fading, so we dropped the rest of it, and walked to the park. We lay in the grass, smoking cigarettes.

Eventually we grew restless, and returned to Tiffany's dad's apartment for more meth. When we arrived at his second-floor landing, the front door was wide open. Inside, the place was trashed. Tiffany was furious. She cussed me out, and hit me several times in the chest. I apologized, but she ignored me, and went out onto the porch to smoke.

It wasn't safe at Tiffany's dad's place anymore, so we walked back to Nate's mom's trailer on the Eastside. On the way, we passed the remnants of the Bro-Hive. The sight of the burnt-out house angered Nate. He gritted his teeth and said he'd get even with Ryan. I wasn't thinking about revenge. I was thinking about Big Dave. I missed him, and felt vulnerable without him.

We stopped at the 7-Eleven for supplies. Our money was getting low, but I still had the forty-dollars from the woman who'd hit me with her car. We bought more beer, cigarettes, and some frozen burritos. I was coming down from the acid, and the left side of my head throbbed.

Screeching tires flooded our ears as we exited the convenient store. A pickup truck bore down on us. I grabbed Tiffany, and got out of harm's way, but Nate got tagged, and tumbled onto the truck's hood. The impact caused the beers under his arm to explode as his body shattered the windshield. The truck stopped, and Nate crumpled down the hood onto the asphalt. Tiffany screamed, and tried to run to Nate, but I held her back as the truck revved its engine. Slowly, Nate sat up. Blood dripped down his face. He looked confused, but then his eyes focused. He reached for the .38, and fired several shots through the busted windshield as the truck peeled out, and crushed Nate under its tires before climbing the curb onto the street. The truck passed, and I saw Ryan behind the wheel. Our eyes met, and he pointed at me before speeding away.

Nate lay crumpled on the ground, laboring to breathe. Blood trickled from his mouth and ears. Tiffany cradled his head in her arms and sobbed as sirens approached. The police made Tiffany and me get down on our stomachs while they searched us. Medics arrived, and Nate disappeared into the back of an ambulance.

Tiffany and I were cuffed, taken to the police station, and interrogated separately. I came clean, and described to the police the events of the last several days. Nate and Ryan had a dispute over a surfboard. Ryan wouldn't pay for the board, so Nate stole Ryan's drugs. Ryan retaliated by burning down the Bro-Hive, which killed Big Dave. Nate returned the favor by texting the police the video of Ryan setting fire to Jerry's Cadillac, and Ryan struck back by trashing Tiffany's dad's apartment, and running down Nate in the 7-Eleven parking lot.

I told them that Tiffany was my girlfriend, and that we were friends with Nate, but that we had just been caught up in the dispute, and hadn't wanted to get involved. When I was done explaining things, they held me for most of the day, but didn't charge me with anything, and eventually I was released.

I didn't know where to go. My mom's was out of the question, so I walked to Tiffany's dad's apartment, but nobody answered the door, so I walked to Nate's mom's trailer, and found Tiffany packing a bag. She said Nate was in critical condition and had been medevacked to Stanford. His mom would be home from work any minute, and they were driving to the hospital. I said I'd go with them, but Tiffany said no. I tried to console her, but she pushed me away.

"Come on Tiffany, you're my girl," I said.

"No, I'm not, and I never was," she said.

"You're fucking him, aren't you?"

"Get out."

"I'm not stupid," I said. "I know what's going on."

"I'm not beholden to you," she said, trying to get by me.

"Yes, you are. You're my girl."

"No, I'm not. Let me go," she screamed.

I grabbed Tiffany by the wrists, but she struggled free, so I hit her, and she collapsed onto the couch. She held her cheek, and kneed me in the balls, so I wrapped my hands around her neck.

"It should have been Nate," I said, looking into her wide eyes as I squeezed. "Not Big Dave. Had it been Nate, everything would be okay. We'd still be together."

Her face turned purple, and spittle dripped from her mouth. I loosened my grip when she went limp, walked into the kitchen, and turned on the stove's gas. Returning to the living room, I sat down by my girl, and lit a smoke.

Burning Snow

I was pissing away the last of my cash on shots and beers in South Madison at the Moccasin when a fat man with a cracked red face and long gray hair sat next to me. Removing his coat, he revealed a faded tie-dyed Grateful Dead T-shirt. After laughing at a Geico commercial on the TV behind the bar, he ordered a shot and a beer.

"Name's Mark," he said.

"Max," I replied.

I'd been in the Berkshires just long enough to slip on the ice and bust my ass. At first, I enjoyed the snow. Big fluffy flakes swirling through the air like the Christmas holidays of my youth, but after a few freezing days, my winter wonderland transformed into a vast expanse of cruddy gray post-apocalyptic tundra.

"Funny thing 'bout a bar," Mark said. "Two strangers sittin' next to each other's buddies after a beer."

Mark bantered on about this and that, and I threw in the obligatory head nod or 'uh-huh' without paying much attention to the conversation. When my beer bottomed out, I reached for my coat.

"Lookin' for a job?" Mark asked. "Shovelin' snow. Could use the help. Ain't runway modelin'. Pays the minimum under the table."

Mark picked me up at my motel room the next day, and we drove to a large house with a long snow-covered driveway near the college. He let me out the truck and said he'd be back in an hour. I shoveled and salted the drive like a bland dinner until a 4x4 with a loud muffler and a snowplow attached to the front stopped across the street. Two heavyset men in parkas and Boston Red Sox caps climbed from the cab.

"You with Mark?" the driver asked.

"We ain't dating," I said.

"This guy being funny?" the passenger asked.

"Wish you'd showed up earlier," I said, motioning to the plow attached to the front of their truck. "Could have saved me some serious work."

They lit cigarettes, and talked amongst themselves before returning to their vehicle. The 4x4 rumbled into the front yard and plowed a heap of snow onto the driveway. The big guys in the truck flipped me off and flung snow and ice at me with the truck's back tires before driving away.

Another car stopped before the driveway as I started in on the fresh mess. A tall slender young woman with long black hair, radiant blue eyes, and pale white skin exited a gold Saturn.

"What happened?" She asked.

"Couple guys got hungry, made a doughnut in the yard."

"Name's Renee."

"Max."

She went inside the house, and returned with a snow shovel. I said it wasn't necessary, but she insisted. I certainly didn't mind the view or the attention.

"Parents' place?" I asked.

"Renting a room. Student at South Madison State."

Mark honked from the street.

"Why's she helpin'?" He asked.

"Wanted to."

"Why ain't you done yet?"

"Couple guys with a plow took it upon themselves to return the snow I'd shoveled to its original resting place."

"Dammit," Mark said. "Hop in."

"Want to grab coffee sometime?" Renee asked when I waved bye.

"Very much so," I said.

"Saturday at the Appalachian Grind," she said. "10:00AM."

"See you there," I said, and climbed into the cab, trying to suppress a smile.

"The Brown Brothers," Mark said at the Moccasin. "Also own a snow removal business. Miserable little shits. Mike Brown Sr.'s their dad, richest son of a bitch in South Madison. Owns the Mountainside Bar and Grill up in Lewisburg."

"How's the steak?" I asked.

"You ain't heard of the Mountainside Bar and Grill? Afterhours parties in the basement, naked women, cocaine, orgies, bondage that sort of thing."

"And they're muscling you out of the snow?" I asked.

"Tryin' to," Mark said with a shrug, revealing a handgun tucked under his shirt. "Mike Jr.'s the fatter of the two brothers, but Toby's also a lardass. You should see their dad. Fattest fuck there ever was."

He went on and on about what creeps the Browns were, but I didn't care. The situation was some ticky-tacky Mickey Mouse bullshit that smacked of preteens fighting for the right to trim Mrs. O'Malley's bush for a quarter. I went along with what Mark was saying without paying much attention, and didn't say no when he offered to buy the next round.

The next morning, somebody knocked on my motel room door. I yelled that I didn't need room service, but the banging continued, so I stumbled out of bed.

"Hurry up Max," Mark said. "Snow ain't shovelin' itself. We got work to do."

I dragged myself into the bathroom, and splashed water on my face. In the cab, Mark handed me a box of doughnuts and a lukewarm coffee.

"This the job?" I asked in front of an aging apartment complex.

"Grabbin' Jolly," Mark said and honked.

A little guy with long greasy brown hair and a tangled beard limped to the truck. I slid over, noticing his swollen nose and blackened eyes.

"Jolly meet Max," Mark said.

We said hello, and drove into Madison. South Madison was a bedraggled string of closed factories and low-income housing, but Madison was an upscale example of what the founding fathers had in mind. Pristine three-story brick mansions lined both sides of the street.

Mark left us at the worksite with shovels and salt. Jolly didn't say much, and I was okay with that, but I was curious about his stupid name, and his recently punched face.

We shoveled our butts off until Mark returned with McDonald's for lunch, and drove away again. I lit a smoke, and Jolly bummed one.

"What happened to your face?" I asked, deciding I didn't care about the origin of his name.

"Shoveling ain't all rainbows and unicorns," he said.

"Should I start worrying about the abominable snowman?" I asked.

"Just the Brown Brothers."

"Ran into them yesterday," I said. "Rich brats trying to edge Mark out the snow game. Their daddy owns a bar up the mountain."

"Bad shit goes down at the Mountainside," Jolly said. "Couple of college girls ended up missing there last year. Let me get another cigarette?"

"Want my wallet too?" I asked, opening my pack.

"Brown Boys are rumored to have ties," Jolly said, lighting the smoke. "What'd you say you used to do?"

"I didn't."

I told Jolly I was a carpenter, flipping houses in Utah, but the work dried up after the crash. None of it was true.

I expected the Brown Brothers to show up and protest our shoveling, but they never did. Neither did our employer. Jolly called Mark's cellphone, but he didn't answer. After waiting in the cold for an hour, we walked toward South Madison. Traversing brown slush on the side of the road, Jolly stuck out his thumb at the passing cars until somebody stopped. The truck was equipped with a gun rack, and the driver wore a camouflage ball cap.

"Thanks for the ride, Howard," Jolly said. "Mark's M.I.A."

"I was drinkin' with him at the Moccasin," Howard said. "Brown Brothers showed. Mark bought 'em drinks, and they poured 'em on his head, dragged him outside, and pistol-whipped him with his own gun. Broke his arm too."

"Why didn't you do something?" Jolly asked.

"You know how it is," Howard said.

After the Dunkin' Donut's drive-thru, Howard dropped me off at my motel. I was tired and sore, so I ate an egg and steak bagel, and drifted off to sleep, watching Sports Center.

I dreamt Gunnar was driving through a snowstorm in the Las Vegas desert. I sat in the passenger seat, pleading for my life. He pulled over in the middle of nowhere, dragged me from the car, and made me dig my own grave in the snow. When I finished the hole, Gunnar shot me in the gut, and I fell backwards into my last resting place. The falling snowflakes turned to cinders as Gunnar shoveled burning snow into the pit.

I woke in a cold sweat, kicking off the blanket. A morning show was on the TV, so I turned it off. I jumped out of bed because I was late for coffee with Renee. I splashed water on my face, and combed my hair. Fragments of the nightmare lingered in my mind when I arrived at the Appalachian Grind.

"Thought you stood me up," Renee said, wearing a low-cut blouse and tight pants.

"You want a croissant or something?" I asked.

"Double Americano with room," she said.

Over steaming drinks, she told me she was from upstate New York, and a junior in the accounting program at the college. I gave her the standard flipping houses in Utah routine when it came time for me to share.

We smoked along Main Street. Churches and real estate offices peppered the strip. Other flavors included a cinema, a playhouse and a bookshop. We stopped at the war memorial, and Renee kissed me. Back at my motel room, we ordered a pizza after sex, and stretched out in bed, naked, smoking and watching shitty television. Some Bogart films were playing at the local cinema, so we dressed, and saw a double feature, but didn't catch much of either film. In the evening, she had to study for an exam, and kissed me goodbye.

I woke early the next day, feeling rested, and ready to shovel the shit out of some snow. Mark never arrived, so

I walked to the Moccasin, hoping to find him on a barstool.

"Seen Mark?" I asked Howard.

"Imagine he's laid up, high as pitch pine" Howard said. "Poor bastard needs to tough it out though, and shovel some drives before the melt."

"I'll do it for him," I said.

"Good man," Howard said, and bought me a shot and a beer.

We stopped at Jolly's after drinks, and Howard honked.

Jolly climbed in the truck, and lit a crack pipe. Howard took a hit. They offered me the glass, but I declined. A snow-covered swing set and various large children's toys sat abandoned in Mark's front yard. A woman with a child on her hip and another hanging from her dress answered the door.

"Afternoon Diane," Howard said. "Came to check on Mark."

"He's asleep," she said.

"Got a couple boys want to shovel for him while he's on the mend."

"Come on in."

The living room was beat to shit, covered in stains and crayon. Mark lumbered into the room with a bandaged forehead, and an arm sling.

"Mornin'," he said, glassy-eyed.

"These boys want to work," Howard said.

"Job at Anderson's cabin," Mark slurred.

"Lewisburg. I know it," Howard said. "Grab your shovels. Let's get movin'."

The road was steep. I thought we'd spin out on the incline, but the snow tires gripped like Velcro. At the Anderson's cabin, Howard left us with the shovels and salt. Amazing how drudgery seems like leisure when you've got a woman on your mind. Work clipped along.

Jolly hit the pipe every twenty minutes. Anderson's neighbor complimented us, and asked if we'd shovel his driveway too. Jolly wanted to go home, but I said yes.

About halfway through the second job, a familiar 4x4 pulled into the driveway. The Brown Brothers exited the truck with baseball bats. Jolly fled behind the Anderson's neighbor's cabin. Can't say I blamed him. He was pretty frail.

"Thought we made it clear, we don't want you shoveling 'round here," Mike Jr. said.

"Plenty snow to go around," I said.

"Let's see if you're still a funny guy after batting practice," Toby said.

Mike Jr. swung his bat. I dodged the blow, and jabbed him in the throat with the shovel blade. Mike Jr. doubled over, wheezing and gurgling. I parried Toby's swing, throwing him off balance. He slipped and fell on his ass. I clocked him hard in the face with the spade. Mike Jr. and Toby slowly got to their feet, and limped to the 4x4.

"You're fucking dead," Toby said.

I lit a cigarette, and waved bye.

"Thought your ass was beat for sure," Jolly said, returning to the front yard. "You whoop 'em?"

"Yep," I said, and took a drag.

"Better watch out," Jolly said. "They're connected."

I was walking to the Appalachian Grind to meet Renee on Saturday morning when I saw him coming out of a bank on Main Street. It couldn't be, but it was. I'd recognize that son of a bitch anywhere. How the hell did Gunnar know I was alive—let alone halfway across the country in Podunk South Madison?

I returned to my motel room, and packed my clothes and .45. I could borrow Mark's truck, and be out of town in under an hour. Somebody knocked. I held my gun at the hip, peeking out the window.

"What the fuck, Max," Renee said. "You never showed. Now I find you here with your thumb up your ass."

"Thanks for the fun, Renee, but I'm the fuck 'em and chuck 'em type," I said.

She slapped my face, and slammed the door.

I felt bad, but it was for the best. I lit a smoke, and started for Mark's house through slushy brown streets. A truck flashed its lights. I reached for my gun.

"Where you been, Max?" Howard said. "Got bad news. Jolly's mom found him dead, drug overdose."

"Damn," I said.

"Heading to Mark's? Hop in."

Thick black smoke filled the sky.

Mark, Diane and their kids stood in the front yard, watching their house burn. Mark's truck was engulfed in flames too. Howard hopped out, leaving the keys in the ignition, so I slid into the driver's seat. I felt bad for Mark and Jolly like maybe I was partially to blame for this mess, but not bad enough to stick around.

"Step outside," Gunnar said through the window, holding a pistol level with my face.

Gunnar disarmed me, and we climbed into the Brown Brother's 4x4. At the Mountainside Bar and Grill, they escorted me through a back door, down a set of stairs, and into a small damp room. Gunnar cracked me on the head with the butt of his gun, and I went limp.

I came to, strapped to a wooden chair, my head throbbing. The basement walls vibrated with techno music.

"Johnny Hall," Gunnar said. "What the hell you doing in this shithole town?"

"I grew up in this shithole town," Toby said.

"No offense," Gunnar said, sticking a knife blade up my nose. "But this ain't exactly Vegas. You pissing off the wrong people again, Johnny. Only you could rise from the grave, and botch a second chance."

A door opened, revealing a blinding light.

"This ain't the bathroom," Toby yelled at somebody, and the door shut.

The blade sliced through my nostril. Blood spurted in time with the pain.

The basement walls melted into my darkened Nevada desert grave. I loosened an arm from under the sand enough to dig out my other arm, and then my face. Stars twinkled overhead as I freed myself. The gunshot wound in my gut leaked, but nothing vital seemed damaged. I walked in moonlight until I saw the neon glow of Las Vegas in the distance.

"Who the hell is it?" Stacy asked from within when I reached her apartment, and knocked on the door. "Johnny, oh my god. Come in. You look like dog shit on fire. What happened?"

Stacy was a stripper I sometimes crashed with. I'd helped her out of enough pickles, and given her enough money when she was in need to know I could trust her. She took me in, cleaned me up, and dressed my wound.

"You better dip, Johnny," Stacy said after I told her Gunnar had buried me for ripping him off. "He'll never stop trying to kill you if he finds out you're still alive."

Stacy gave me a ride to the depot, and I boarded the first leviathan out of town.

The basement walls, the techno music and the horrible pain in my nose reanimated. I sat alone in the darkness. Through a purple gloom, a door opened. The silhouette of a woman twinkled with a thousand tiny constellations.

"Max?" A celestial voice whispered, untying my wrists and legs. "Let's get you out of here."

"Stacy?" I asked as she led me up the stairs, and out the back door.

"Who's Stacy? I have to get back before they notice," Renee said, her body shimmering with glitter in the moonlight as she descended the stairs.

I staggered toward the tree line at the edge of the parking lot. Angry voices emanated behind me, followed by gunshots. I disappeared into the forest, and stopped to catch my breath. My side burned, and blood smeared my hand when I touched my waist.

"Come back, Johnny," Gunnar said from the parking lot. "Got your lady friend. Come back, or we'll feed her to Mike Sr."

The snow was deep. The cold brought back my senses. I stayed out of sight in the trees, trying not to think about my wounds, or what Gunnar meant by feeding Renee to the Brown Boys' dad. Hypothermia was setting in as I reached the Moccasin. My mutilated face was blue and my teeth rattled like a trestle. Howard and Mark sat at the end of the bar. Mark's head lay on the counter, surrounded by a traffic jam of empty shot glasses.

"What the hell happened?" Howard asked.

"He can't be in here looking like that," the bartender said.

Howard threw cash on the bar, and dragged Mark from the tavern to his truck. I cranked on the heater.

"Brown Brothers give you that nose job?" Howard asked.

"What do you know about Mike Sr.?"

"Has a penchant for the college girls. Rumored to be into some kinky shit. He was a suspect when those two women went missing. Never found 'em either. You want a ride to the hospital?"

"A woman I know is in trouble," I said. "I need a gun."

Howard nodded, and drove us to his house. Animal busts hung on the walls. Mark snored on the couch. Howard gave me a roll of gauze.

"You kill these animals?" I asked.

"Most of 'em," he said. "Pops got a few."

"Live alone?" I asked.

"Wife left about a year ago. It was drinking or her. Easy choice. Get that tape on your nose. Tired of looking at your busted face."

Howard led me into a backroom.

"This here's a .30-06 Springfield," he said. "I can wipe a buck's ass from a thousand yards with this bad boy. Take this Russian AEK-971 assault rifle, and this M9 Beretta. Put this .38 in your boot."

"Why you doing this for me?" I asked.

"Jolly didn't die from an overdose, and Mark's place didn't burn down by accident. Browns' been terrorizing South Madison for far too long. We've needed a crazy son of a bitch like you to come along, and clean house for some time."

"Got any gas?" I asked.

On the drive, we didn't talk. My mind wandered to pancakes and coffee at an all-night diner on the Vegas strip.

"Pass the syrup," Fred said. "You're paler than a ghost. First kill is always the hardest. It gets easier from here on out. Second nature."

"You don't think any less of me 'cause I puked?" I asked.

"Hell no," he laughed. "If memory serves, I chunked my first time too. The thing you need to understand now is that by killing that man, you've signed your own death certificate."

"What?"

"There's now a bullet with your name on it. Natural progression of the trade," Fred said. "I got one with my name on it too."

A few months later, Fred's prophecy came true, and his bullet found its way through his temple, during a botched bank robbery.

A truck idled in the middle of the road after the turnoff to the Mountainside Bar and Grill. Two men leaned against the hood. I hid in the back of the cab.

"Evening, boys," Howard said, rolling down the window. "Why you in the middle of the road?"

"None of your goddamn business," one of the men said, shining a flashlight at Howard's face. "What you doing here?"

"Hoping to grab a burger, and a side of pussy," Howard said.

"Restaurant's closed," the man said. "Step out the truck."

"Why?" Howard asked.

"Just step the fuck out," the man said pointing a gun at Howard.

I sat up, and fired four shots through the window. Both men dropped to the ground, each with two bullet holes in the forehead.

"Jesus Christ," Howard said.

"Where?" I asked.

We drove around the dead men and their truck. In the restaurant's parking lot, somebody opened fire. I ducked out of the cab with the guns and gas can. A hail of gunfire blasted through the restaurant's front window. A bullet struck my shoulder. I opened fire with the assault rifle, and made my way through the front door.

The bar was empty, so I poured gasoline over the counter, and lit a match. A bullet nicked my ear. I walked into the kitchen. Mike Jr. fumbled with a jammed pistol. I raised the M9 to his head, and heat ripped through my lower back, followed by a deafening crack, lightening before thunder. I dropped to my knees.

"I'll kill you a thousand times if I have to," Gunnar said, putting a gun to my head.

"Stop burying me alive, and you won't have to," I said as the flames ate away at the ceiling.

"See you in hell, Johnny," Gunnar said as the flames found the gas line, and an exploding fireball knocked us off our feet.

The roof collapsed, and burning debris crashed down around me. I sat up, looking for Gunnar as snowflakes fell through the hole in the roof, mingling with the flames. Through the smoke, I saw Gunnar's body lying on the floor. His head crushed under a blazing wooden beam.

Crawling beneath thick black smoke, I made my way down the stairs into the basement, passing several tables and a stripper pole. I found Renee tied to a board, and covered in lacerations. A massive naked fat man with clothespins clipped to his nipples and genitals held a knife to Renee's throat. He was a spitting image of his boys only older, and fatter—much fatter. The fire ate away at the walls.

"Drop the knife, asshole," I said, pointing the M9 at Mike Sr.

He stabbed Renee in the gut as I unloaded my weapon.

Mike Sr. collapsed in a fat heap of bullet holes on the floor. Renee screamed in agony as I untied her. Smoke and flames filled the room. We stumbled up the backstairs into the snow.

My breathing grew shallow. The restaurant was completely engulfed in flames. Several sharp pains ripped through my chest. I went down on my knees as I saw the Brown Brothers approaching with rifles.

More gunshots sounded, and I realized there was crossfire. Toby went down, and Mike Jr. dragged him behind a car. The barrel of a .30-06 peeked from the window of Howard's truck across the parking lot. Mike Jr. returned fire, and Howard slumped over the steering wheel onto the horn.

Renee helped me to my feet, and we stumbled into the timberline. Blood stained the snow behind us as we staggered through the drift. At a small clearing, we rested on a fallen log.

I sank into Renee's arms.

"I strip to help pay for college," Renee said.

"I knew there was something I liked about you," I said, and a gunshot knocked her off the log.

"Toby's dead," Mike Jr. said, covered in blood, and holding a pistol.

"So is your pervert dad."

He raised his gun as I pulled the .38 from my boot, and sent Mike Jr. across the river Styx to join his family as two bullets from his gun, one named Johnny Hall and the other named Max, tore through my chest.

Moonlight illuminated Renee's body. The glitter on her breasts twinkled through the blood like a thousand tiny stars across a red sky. I crawled through the snow, and kissed her blue lips as though she would wake, and we'd live happily ever after, but this sure as hell ain't no fairytale.

All that Nighttime

A warm breeze swept along the water as the old lady and her hulking adult son wheeled the food cart onto the river path. A puff of steam rose from the cauldron as the old woman removed a sweaty lid and stirred the broth. Her gigantic son set up a folding table and carefully organized several rows of empty paper cups. She ladled the hot soup into the small receptacles, and said a prayer.

The homeless men and women along the shoreline of the San Lorenzo crawled from their tattered sleeping bags atop cardboard, and stretched their tired and sore limbs. Longing for warm beds, hot coffee, and a high strong enough to numb the pain, the transients slowly made their way toward the old soup lady's cart.

A loud bang from the riverbank cut Happy from a dream about his mother. He didn't want to look in the casket, but an uncle grabbed him by the scruff and made him. His mother's expression was peaceful. Happy had never seen her so content in life. Her eyes opened. She sat up, vomiting blood and pointing at Happy as the booming sound cracked across the sky, rousing him from sleep. He rubbed the sweat off his face, stretched his arms, and pulled his wavy red hair back into a ponytail.

Gristle sat next to him with a backpack over his shoulder, stabbing a syringe into a grapefruit-sized abscess on his right thigh, filling the needle with pus, and squirting the bloody suppuration into an empty Coke can.

"You were talking in your sleep," Gristle said. "Screaming, mommy."

"Shit," Happy said with a yawn. "Gonna get some soup."

"You see Rip Off Ronny there, tell him I want my forty bucks," Gristle said, jabbing the syringe back into his festering leg.

Happy crossed the bridge, and made his way to the soup line. Spider and Nancy queued up behind him. Spider's head was shaved and covered with faded blue tattoos. Various metal studs pierced his face. Nancy wore a skimpy red skirt and a stained white tank top. Her makeup was smudged, and her bleached blonde hair was tangled in frizzy knots. Spider kept looking over his shoulder with shifty eyes.

"Seen Ronny?" Happy asked.

"Not for a couple days," Spider said nervously, lifting his shirt, and flashing a handgun tucked into his waistband. "But when I do, gonna fuck him up bad. Owes me a hundo."

"Try Heady. He's always hanging with Ronny," Nancy said, and Spider gave her a savage glare.

"Got any daytime?" Spider asked.

"Know where to get some," Happy said. "Got money?"

"Got something better," Nancy said, grabbing her breasts.

"When you feed others, you feed Christ," the old lady said, and her ogre son handed each of them a cup of warm nourishment.

Spider and Nancy sipped from their paper cups, and followed Happy over the bridge to Gristle's encampment. Gristle climbed to his feet, and licked his lips as Nancy helped him into the brush down by the river. Happy and Spider sat on a dirty piece of cardboard, snorting Happy's meth. Spider rambled on about what he would do to Rip Off Ronny if somebody else didn't find him first. Happy's mother walked out of the bushes, holding the right side of her face.

"She likes it rough," Gristle said, limping to the cardboard.

"Bastard hit me," Nancy said.

Spider grabbed the barrel of his gun, and smashed the butt against Gristle's head. Gristle dropped like a grubby bowling ball. Nancy yanked Gristle's backpack off his shoulder, and kicked him in the face. Gristle flopped on the ground like a fish out of water, foaming at the mouth like a mangy dog.

"I'll kill him," Spider said, pointing the gun at Gristle, and bouncing from foot to foot.

"Do it," Happy's mother said. "He beats women."

"Mom," Happy said.

"Fuck is wrong with you?" Spider asked, pressing the gun to Happy's forehead. "She ain't your momma, but I'll be your daddy."

Nancy looked inside the backpack, and her eyes filled her face.

"Spider, honey, we hit the jackpot," Nancy said. "Ronny wasn't full of shit for once."

"Don't come looking for us," Spider said, backing away from the encampment with Nancy. "Or I'll shoot your ass."

41

"You okay?" Happy asked Gristle when his wits returned.

"Spider's a dead man," Gristle said, holding his head as blood dripped down his face.

"Gristle," Happy said with a shiver. "I'm getting sick."

"Me too," Gristle said, retrieving a crowbar and a brown paper bag from the bushes.

Happy helped Gristle trek to a green metal needle disposal bin near the river path. Gristle slid the crowbar through the padlock, and torqued until the steel snapped. The door popped open, and Gristle reached into the large receptacle, removing a handful of bloody gauze and used syringes. Happy held open the brown bag, and Gristle placed the needles in the paper sack.

Back at camp, Gristle and Happy disassembled the syringes, and gathered the leftover blood and heroin from each needle until they had enough to shoot. The effect of the leftovers was weak, but it quelled the withdrawal symptoms. Happy lay on his back with his hands behind his neck, looking up at his mother's head floating along with the clouds. Her curly red hair slithered like snakes. Gristle nudged the dreamer, and the matriarchal skull in the sky popped like a balloon.

"Come on, mama's boy," Gristle said. "Time we see Howie."

"Fuck that guy."

Several months ago, Howie savagely beat Happy with a wrench when Happy's meth money came up short. Since the incident, Happy avoided the drug dealer, but managed to stay high on Howie's supply by befriending Howie's only other pusher, Gristle.

Blood coagulated in Gristle's greasy hair. He stopped every few blocks to rub his decrepit leg, and complain about the pain. Pedestrians crossed the street to avoid him. At an old rundown, blue paint-chipped, two-story

Victorian house near the high school, Gristle and Happy entered the backyard through a warped wooden gate. Rusty metal junk piles and weeds gone to seed suffocated the ground.

"Fuck happened to you?" A tiny shirtless albino hunchback with tattooed sleeves and bleached blonde dreadlocks asked Gristle in a high-pitched voice at the garage door.

"I need a gun, Howie," Gristle said.

"Where's my money?" Howie asked. "And don't give me any bullshit. If you ain't got it, I want my shit back."

"Spider got it."

"All of it?" Howie asked.

"That piece of shit, Rip Off Ronny, tipped him off that I was holding. Give me the gun, and I'll get it back," Gristle said.

Howie grabbed a wrench from a disorganized toolbox, and hurled it at Gristle's head. The wrench missed Gristle, but hit Happy in the sternum. Happy bent over, crossing his arms over his chest, and gasped for air. Gristle stumbled into the albino hunchback, shoving him into a corner. Howie raised his hands, pleading not to be hurt.

"The Gun, Howie," Gristle said.

Howie cussed under his breath, waddling to a desk cluttered with plastic bottles filled with his piss. He dug around in a drawer, tossing pornography magazines on the floor until he found the weapon.

"I shouldn't lend it to you," Howie said. "I should shoot you with it for losing my product."

In Howie's hand, the snub-nose .38 looked massive, but in Gristle's hand, it looked small. Gristle opened the chamber, and checked for bullets.

"You all right, Happy?" Gristle asked. "Gonna be hard getting around without you."

"Give me a minute," Happy said, and vomited on the floor.

"Better get my stuff back," Howie said. "You know what that shit's cut with."

Gristle and Happy returned to the river path. Sweat dripped from Gristle's stubbly chin as he dragged along his infected leg. Happy's chest ached as he labored for breath. Behind a fenced off city generator near the river path, they sat in the dirt, and snorted the last of Happy's meth. A coffin floated on the river. Happy rubbed his eyes, and the sarcophagus turned into a log drifting downstream.

Near a yoga studio on Front Street, a congregation of transients sat in a drum circle, beating bongos out of time while hippies danced topless. Gristle limped through the cacophony, and grabbed a percussive street urchin named Heady by the hood of his dirty black sweater.

"What the fuck?" Heady asked against the anti-rhythmic beats.

"Where's Spider?" Gristle asked, flashing the .38.

"This about Ronny?" Heady asked. "You got somewhere else we can go?"

Heady followed Gristle and Happy. The drumming sound carried along with the breeze as the homeless men crossed the bridge over the San Lorenzo to Gristle's encampment. Heady spastically played his bongo along with the distant circle.

"Start talking," Gristle said, pointing the pistol at Heady.

"You hear that gunshot this morning down by the river?" Heady asked.

"I heard it," Gristle said.

"Spider shot Ronny," Heady said. "I seen the body."

"Where?" Gristle asked, and they followed Heady into the brush.

Near a sandy inlet on the river's edge, Heady pointed to some bushes. Matted weeds and bloodstains dotted the shoreline, but Ronny's corpse was nowhere to be found.

"Ronny's body was here this morning," Heady said.

"Maybe the cops found it," Happy said.

"This place would be closed off, and swarming with pigs," Gristle said. "You're full of shit, Heady. Where's Spider?"

"I seen Ronny laying there dead as god," Heady said.

"Fuck is Spider?" Gristle asked, putting the gun to Heady's head.

"Saw him about an hour ago," Heady said. "Gave me some shit he owed me to keep quiet."

"Where. Is. He?"

"Motel in the flats," Heady said.

"Which one?"

"I don't know," Heady said, handing Gristle a little baggy. "Take what Spider gave me man. Just leave me alone."

"Get the fuck out of here," Gristle said, and Heady took off running.

Gristle and Happy found a little clearing, and set about cooking and shooting Heady's heroin.

"That's definitely Howie's shit," Gristle said, lying back in the weeds.

"You smell that?" Happy asked, climbing to his feet.

Happy wandered through the brush until he saw a tent hidden in the thicket. Out front, his mother stirred a pot of steaming broth over a fire. He was about to greet her when somebody grabbed him by the shoulder.

"What the fuck," Gristle said. "Making me follow you with a bum leg through the jungle. Leave that old soup lady alone. She ain't your mom. Let's get a move on. I want to find Spider and that double-crosser Ronny before sundown."

Gristle and Happy stopped at a 7-Eleven, and Happy bought two packs of cigarettes from his mother. He gave one pack to Gristle, and they hobbled to a row of run-down motels near the Little Caesars. A young prostitute they didn't recognize in a miniskirt stood on the corner near a taqueria. Scabs and black eyes riddled her face.

"Got a dollar?" She asked. "Trying to get back to Sacramento."

"Seen a man with a tattooed face?" Gristle asked, offering her a cigarette and a light.

"Maybe," she said. "Sure, you don't got a dollar?"

"Where?" Gristle asked.

"Help me out," she said. "I'm stranded."

"Where?" Gristle repeated, snatching the lit cigarette from her painted lips, grabbing her by the hair, and holding the burning ember near her swollen eye.

"Stop," she pleaded.

"He's an ugly tattooed motherfucker with a bunch of metal shit in his face," Gristle said, moving the cigarette closer to her pupil. "Tell me where you seen him."

"There," she said, pointing to a row of seedy motel rooms. "Asked me if I wanted to party, but his dumb ass bitch got hella pissed."

"Which room?"

"I don't know," she said. "Let go."

Gristle threw her to the ground. Happy gave her a dollar, but his mother knocked the money out of his hand into the gutter.

Gristle knocked on the first door, and a fat man in boxers answered.

"Yeah?" He asked.

"Spider in there?" Gristle asked.

"Who?" The fat man asked.

"A Tattooed motherfucker."

"Sounds like the prick next door. Tell him to turn down his goddamn TV," the fat man said.

Nobody answered when Gristle knocked, so he shouldered the hollow wooden door until it splintered, and he gained entry. Spider and Nancy lay pale, slack-jawed and motionless on the bed. Syringes dangled from their arms. The television blared a crime show. Happy leaned over Nancy, closed his mother's eyes, and kissed her cheek.

"Was a baseball this morning," Gristle said, removing a golf ball of tar from his backpack.

Leaving the flats, Gristle's infected leg went numb, so he latched onto Happy's shoulder for support as the long rays of the sunset stretched their shadows across the street.

"You didn't tell me you had all that nighttime," Happy said back at Gristle's encampment.

"Didn't want you nagging me," Gristle said, drawing pus from his abscess with a syringe.

"You gonna see a doctor about your leg?" Happy asked.

Happy shared a needle with Gristle, and drifted into unconsciousness. His mother's head floated peacefully in the nighttime sky as darkness fluttered in the corners of his vision. Before long, there was nothing except the gentle sound of the river flowing by. Happy woke alone with a shiver as a full moon broke free from the clouds, illuminating the brush. The sound of his mother's voice floated through the air on the cold breeze.

By moonlight, Happy followed her trancelike voice down a brambly trail of matted weeds along the San Lorenzo until he came to a clearing by the shore.

"Mom," Happy said as he stepped from the brush into the encampment.

"When you feed others, you feed Christ," the old soup lady said, kneeling in supplication next to a severed and purulent leg as her ogre son stirred a steaming cauldron of soup with a stick.

47

Red Rocks

I rented a little house in midtown. Instead of a lawn, the yard had those shitty red rocks out front, which suited me just fine because my meth lab was fronting as a residential home, so I didn't want the hassle of lawn maintenance. My crew worked nights and early mornings, concocting crystal in the rental's bathroom. Ferral was my chemist. He was a timid man, balding with long strips of thin blonde hair tied back in a ponytail. Donny and Rachael made runs for me at the various drugstores, buying the required common household supplies. Donny was twenty years old, and from Sacramento. His cheeks were covered in freckles and acne. Rachael was twenty-two and from somewhere in Southern California. At a distance, she looked pretty, but upon closer inspection, too much makeup failed to conceal red blotches on her face.

I grabbed my car keys for a McDonald's run. I kept my crew well fed, and not because I was a nice guy. If somebody wasn't eating, they were getting high, and that was a no-no. As I left the house, I noticed a toppled gray statue of a cherub, holding a birdbath in the front yard. I crunched through the red rocks, and helped the angel back to its feet before unlocking the door of my pickup truck.

Everybody wants the American dream. A big house, a fast car, a blonde wife with big tits, and a of couple future Olympians for kids, and I'm no different only I'm on the fast track to prosperity. What all these hardworking shlubs, toiling nine-to-five, don't comprehend is they'll never climb that mountain. Hard work is the path to debt and nowhere town, enslavement. The only people reaching the promised land are the ones pulling the rug out from under the suckers. And that's me, yanking like hell.

Upon returning home from McDonald's, I noticed a commercial van parked in front of the house. Walking through the red rocks with greasy fast-food bags, a bad premonition enveloped me. I envisioned half a dozen feds crammed in the back, tapping my phone line.

A beautiful woman stepped down from the stoop of my rental. She looked fortyish with long silky blonde hair. The pale-yellow power suit she wore struggled against her vivacious curves. She smiled as we passed, her high heels clacking along the path, her hips swaying to and fro.

"Who was that?" I asked, coming through the door as Ferral and Rachael swarmed the McDonald's bags.

"Said her name's Sally. Sells vacuum cleaners," Donny said, lighting a cigarette.

"She's giving us a free demonstration."

"With the vacuum?" I asked, looking at the rancid floor.

Soda spills and cigarette ash blackened the mauve-colored carpet. Dollar store dishes and plates dominated the sink and kitchen counters. Refuse from supplies littered the bedroom. Streamlining prosperity was by no means clean. The only immaculate area in the house was Ferral's bathroom laboratory.

"She'll be back in twenty minutes to demonstrate the cleaning power of the … what did she call it?" Donny asked, flicking cigarette ash onto the carpet. "The Hydro-Vac."

"It's one of those water jobs," Rachael said.

"I don't care if it runs on vaporized plutonium," I said.

"That would be a serious fire hazard," Ferral interjected, licking his fingers.

"I don't give a shit," I said, smashing an unwrapped Egg McMuffin with my fist. "Why didn't you follow procedural protocol, and tell her thank you, but we aren't interested?"

"Procedural protocol? You sound like my old manager at Wal-Mart," Donny said.

"Donny thought she was cute," Rachael said between slurps of orange juice.

"Look at this disgusting carpet," Donny said. "Why not have a beautiful mature woman clean it for us?"

"Because she might not really sell vacuums, dumbass," I said, stuffing a sausage biscuit into my mouth, and washing the dryness down with carton milk.

"No way," Donny said, lighting a cigarette. "A babe that smoking. No way she's a pig."

"Did you see the van out front?" I asked. "Classic stakeout wagon."

"You're paranoid," Donny said, flicking his cigarette ash on the carpet.

"Eat something," I said. "Ain't you hungry?"

"Maybe if you hadn't smashed my food," Donny said unwrapping the flattened Egg McMuffin.

"You better be right about her," I said.

"Find out in twenty minutes."

"Getting low on supplies," Ferral said. "Time for a run."

"You heard the man," I said to Donny and Rachael. "Get to work, and be smart about it. Change up the stores you hit. Don't draw suspicion."

"What about our meal?" Rachael asked, rubbing her stomach.

"It'll be waiting for you when you get back," I said.

"Cold McDonald's," Rachael said. "Brutal."

Donny lingered in the living room while Rachael exited the backdoor, and pedaled away on her bicycle.

"Get going," I said.

"What about Sally?" Donny asked.

"What about her?"

"I want to see her vacuum the floor."

"She ain't getting through the front door, Donny," I said. "I'm sending her ass packing the moment she returns. Now get on your bike, and do your job."

"But what about the vacuum? I bet it's heavy, and she'll have carried it up the porch."

I lit a cigarette, and stared at the floor. Reluctantly, Donny slung his pack over his shoulder, and slammed the backdoor. That kid was standing frontline for an ass whooping. One more fuck up like that and he was toast. I'd gone through countless dumbshits in this operation, and Donny was no different. I couldn't understand why people like him struggled with the simplest of tasks. If he didn't pull his head out of his rear, I'd kick him to the curb, and find another stooge.

To calm myself, I sat in a cracked and plastic off-white lawn chair, and strummed several songs by the Beatles on my Martin Rosewood Grand while smoking. The guitar was an heirloom handed down from my grandfather. Besides money, it was the only thing I cared about in this world. Twenty minutes passed, and my mind shifted to cashing in my chips. The first thing I'd do is fix my teeth. Chicks dig straight teeth. Thinking about ladies reminded me of the vacuum broad. Maybe she wasn't a cop. Maybe she was a nymphomaniac. Maybe she went door to door fucking men. Hell, if Donny returned and found me bedding down with the vacuum lady, it'd teach him a lesson far more powerful than any beating.

"Did Sally come back?" Donny asked when he returned from his errand.

"If you ever invite a stranger inside again, or draw attention to us by slamming another door in this house, I will trounce the living piss out of you and kick your ass to the curb. Got it?"

Donny didn't like what I was saying, but I wasn't running a feel-good resort. He stormed into the bedroom, and I returned to the lawn chair, my grandfather's guitar, and the cigarettes. I was working my way through 'Black Bird' when somebody knocked on the front door.

"Who's that?" Donny asked, reappearing in the living room.

"How the hell should I know," I said, setting down my guitar, and tucking my gun into my waistband.

I opened the door, expecting a gorgeous blonde, but instead a tall, barrel chested man, wearing boots, blue jeans, a white collared shirt and a cowboy hat, loomed in the doorjamb, holding a massive vacuum. Before I could speak, he stepped passed me into the living room.

"Whooee," the cowboy said with a whistle. "Damn if this ain't the dirtiest rug west of the Mississippi. Like it's been drowned in motor oil or something. Howdy partner, name's Carl. I'm sure glad you signed up for our free carpet cleaning demonstration this evening because this floor will test the limits of a vacuum, but I tell you what. When you see the Hydro-Vac's results, you ain't gonna be able to refuse my offer, no way, no how. You'll be so impressed; you'll buy another one for your mama."

52

"We don't need a demonstration," I said, hoping I wouldn't have to use my gun. "Thank you. Be on your way."

"Hold on there a minute, partner," Carl said, plugging the chord into the wall socket. "You know I'll do you square. Won't take but a few minutes, and I'll have these badlands looking like the pastures of heaven in no time. They say you can't polish a turd, but boy, I tell you what."

"Where's Sally?" Donny asked as Carl turned on the vacuum.

The Hydro-Vac sounded like a Boeing 747 coming in for a landing. A torrent of hot air burst forth from an exhaust valve like jet propulsion, knocking Carl's cowboy hat off the back of his head. His head was bald and lumpy with bright red patches on his scalp like cracks in a dry riverbed.

Ferral and Rachael came into the living room upon hearing the vacuum's sonic boom. We gathered around the carpet's perimeter, watching the cowboy work. Sweat dripped from his brow as he wrangled the mechanical beast. I figured he'd only plow a small patch of toxic waste, but Carl pushed that cleaner up and down the entire width and length of the living room.

We pitched in, moving lawn chairs so he wouldn't miss any spots. The vacuum's first attempt morphed the carpet from tar black to ash gray, but on the second flyby, the floor regained its original mauve luster. The cowboy arched his back, and stepped on the cleaner's on/off switch. The growling motor slowed until silent. Carl wiped the sweat from his forehead, and searched for his cowboy hat. Donny handed it to him.

"Thanks, boy," Carl said, unplugging the vacuum. "What do you think? That was some clean job. I didn't know the carpet was purple before the Hydro-Vac washed out all that crud, did you? Now it sparkles like new, and it's all thanks to the magic of this incredible marvel of the modern world."

"Carpet looks nice," I admitted.

"Glad to hear it," Carl said, reaching out to shake my hand and exposing a massive sweat stain under his armpit. "This machine can be yours for eight easy payments of one hundred dollars, and you'll never have to go back to living atop a tar pit again. Don't that sound nice? I know you ain't got no vacuum in here. Take ahold of this beast."

I didn't want to touch the vacuum, but the slick-talking cowboy thrust the hose into my grip.

"Now you got the eighth wonder of the world in the palm of your hand."

"I'm not buying this vacuum," I said, handing him back the nozzle."

"That's cold, mister," he said, tipping his hat back. "I bust my butt floating your floor, and you do me like that? How you missing out on this spectacular deal? Tell you what. Act now, I'll knock fifty bucks off the price and throw in a Hydro-Handheld for free."

"I'll pass," I said. "Now if you'll be on your way, I'd appreciate it."

"Well, shiit," Carl said, looking around the room. "You play guitar?"

"A little."

"Know any country?"

"Hank Williams," I said.

"That's my bread and butter,"

I strummed the chords to "Long Gone Lonesome Blues," and Carl yodeled the lyrics.

"You sing in a band?" I asked when the song ended.

"Nah, just karaoke every chance I get," Carl said. "You sure you won't buy this here vacuum?"

"Positive," I said.

"Shiit," Carl said with a sigh. "Just another no good, worthless, cheap ass, son of a bitch."

"Pardon?" I asked, reaching for my pistol.

Before I drew, a shotgun appeared in my face.

"Fucking move," Rachael said. "And I'll blow off your goddamn head."

"Nice work, baby girl," Carl said. "Your mama raised you right."

"This prick's your dad?" I asked.

"I'm warning you. Don't move," she said. "You're a real piece of shit. And I'd have no problem offing you."

Carl slugged me in the gut, knocking me to the floor. It felt damp and smelled scented. He disarmed me and kicked me in the ribs.

"Do exactly what we say. Be a shame to dirty this freshly cleaned carpet," Carl said. "Not sure how well the Hydro works on brains."

Rachael made Donny and Ferral stand in the corner with their hands up, facing the wall.

"Don't kill me," Donny said. "I don't want to die."

"Then cooperation is imperative," Carl said.

"Yes, sir," Donny said, peeing his pants.

The front door opened, and the vacuum saleswoman entered with rope.

"Hi, mama," Rachael said, and helped Carl hogtie me like a calf at the rodeo.

"Hi, baby girl," the vacuum saleslady said.

"Parents?" I asked Rachel.

"Yep, and Rachael ain't my real name, neither," she said in a southern drawl.

"And you're not from Southern California."

"I'm not from California, but I'm from the South."

"You done good, baby girl," the vacuum saleslady said. "Mama's real proud."

"So's Pa," Carl said. "Be a sweetheart and gather up the goodies."

Rachael, or whatever her name really was, ran into the bedroom, and came back with two large clear Ziploc bags filled with crystal meth.

"Well, shiit," Carl said. "You boys been busy. Now where's the cash?"

"He knows," Rachael said, pointing at me.

Carl kicked me in the chest, and smashed me in the face with the butt of my own gun.

"Start talking."

"Go fuck yourself," I said, dripping blood onto the carpet.

"What if I kill him?" Carl said putting the gun to the back of Donny's head.

"Please don't," Donny pleaded.

"I don't give a shit about the kid," I said. "He's the one let you in."

"That's not entirely true," Carl said, pointing the gun at Ferral. "Where's the money, or your chemist gets a hole in his noodle."

"I can find another chemist," I said.

"Then what about this here guitar?" Carl asked. "Be a shame to break it on your head."

"There's a heating vent on the floor in the bedroom. Unscrew the grate, and feel around," I said, and Rachael disappeared into the bedroom.

Several moments passed, and Rachael returned with several large wads of cash.

"That it?" Carl asked, and kicked me in the ribs again.

"Yeah, now put down my guitar."

"I said it'd be a shame to break your head with it. I didn't say I'd put it down. Now don't take it too personal. You got a hell of a clean carpet out the deal, and that's something you can be proud of."

"Come on, little bro," Rachael said, and Donny turned around.

"She's your sister?" I asked.

"The boy's good ain't he," Carl said.

"Thanks, pa," Donny said, shedding his California accent, and kicking me in the ribs. "Who's ass-whooping who, huh?"

"Least I didn't piss my pants," I said when the kicking stopped.

"I didn't neither," Donny said. "I used a bottle of water to make it look real."

"Like I said, the boy's good."

"How about you Ferral?" I asked. "You related to these assholes?"

"No, but they got a real laboratory. No more working out of the toilet for me."

"Don't get any wild hairs, and come looking for us," Carl said as Donny stretched out a long piece of duct tape.

Sally removed the floor attachment to the vacuum. Rachael thrust the nozzle into my mouth, and Donny taped it to my head. Carl picked up my guitar, and put his cowboy boot on the vacuum's on/off switch.

"Damn, this sure is a nice picker," Carl said. "I power up the Hydro-Vac, and your lungs, stomach, intestines and soul become the property of this here vacuum. Last chance to buy this beaut. Got a hell of a suction."

"Okay," I said as best I could with a metal hose jammed into my mouth.

"Well, shiit," Carl said. "Looks to me like we got ourselves another satisfied customer."

Carl raised his boot to stomp the vacuum's on/off switch. I winced at the thought of my organs leaving my body in such a violent manner, but instead, Carl stepped back, and strummed my grandfather's guitar.

"She's long gone, and I'm lonesome and blue," he yodeled. "Awful fine picker."

The cowboy and his family, my guitar, my meth, my money, and my chemist exited the house. Donny slammed the front door. For a moment, there was silence, but then the grinding sound of boots, walking across red rocks, crushed the skeletal remains of my American Dream into an immaculate carpet.

Eddie Spaghetti

"Scary, cover the hippy cashier," Screw said in the van, pulling the ski mask down over his face, obscuring the faded blue swastika tattoo on his cheek. "He so much as farts, you put a bullet in his head."

"I've never fired a gun before," Scary said, holding the .45 at Screw's chest.

"Point it at the Phish fan behind the counter when we get inside, not at me," Screw said, pushing the barrel away. "Smoky Dave."

"Yep," Smoky Dave said, throwing the butt of his cigarette out the van's window.

"Herd the stoners into a corner. If somebody starts acting like John Wayne, blast 'em. I'll go first, and cut down that big security guard motherfucker."

"We won't actually shoot nobody will we?" Scary asked, pulling the bill of her black ball cap low over her eyes.

"I fuckin' hope so," Smoky Dave said behind a hockey mask, sliding two shells into the shotgun.

Screw gave Smoky Dave a confidential look that put Scary ill at ease like they knew something important she didn't. Exiting the van, they approached the pot dispensary.

"Eddie. Eddie Spaghetti. His meatballs are ready," Scary said under her breath, and rubbed the aluminum tab torn from a soda can in her pocket.

Screw bounded through the front door, and smashed the massive security guard in the head with the butt of his Glock, wilting the big man like a thirsty plant.

"Everybody, face the wall," Smoky Dave said, kicking open the second door, ripping one into the ceiling, and counting four scared shitless customers.

"Hands up," Scary said, pointing the .45 at the white hippy with dreadlocks behind the counter.

"Be cool lady," the hippy cashier said, squinting at her. "Be cool."

"I said get your hands up," Scary said.

"I know you," the hippy said. "We went to school together. You were what's-his-name's girl."

"Shut up," Scary said.

"You just signed your death warrant," Screw said, and squeezed the trigger.

The hippy flopped around on the floor as blood gushed from the side of his head. Panicked sobs and mournful cries erupted from the patrons. Two middle-eastern men hugged each other, and a young white woman with tattooed sleeves and plugs in her earlobes, crossed herself, and tried to look for heaven in the ceiling. An older woman in a red power suit and matching pumps stood frozen in a defiant stance.

Scary winced at the dead hippy on the ground. His name was Ricky Fred. She remembered ditching P.E. to smoke weed with him in his V.W. Bug during freshman year. He felt her up, so she punched him in the balls. Scary hated him for that, but didn't wish him dead. There was only one person she wished death on.

"Quiet down, or I start shooting," Smoky Dave said to the costumers.

"I'm not scared of you," the woman in red said, coming to life. "I haven't survived breast cancer to be killed by some punk at a stickup."

"Lady, I swear to God if you don't turn around, and put your face against the wall, I will blow your fuckin' head off," Smoky Dave said.

"You will not," the woman said, clutching her purse. "I'm leaving, and don't try to stop me."

▼▼▼

Scary woke in a large city planter box in front of the public library with a raging headache.

"Eddie. Eddie Spaghetti. His meatballs are ready," she said, and felt the aluminum tab in her pocket before plodding downtown and scrounging through public ashtrays to assuage her nicotine addiction.

"Scary," Smoky Dave said, handing her a cigarette and a matchbook. "Where you been?"

She lit the smoke, and looked at her reflection in a storefront window. Her blue hair was pulled back exposing brown roots. Her face was swollen, sunburnt, and covered in runny scabs. Smoky Dave wore a crusty black leather jacket, and no shirt underneath. His long dark hair dangled in front of his face, obscuring his features.

"Nowhere."

"Got a job for you."

"I don't suck dick."

"It ain't like that," Smoky Dave said, and inhaled from a vape pen. "You know my buddy, Screw?"

"No."

"Skinhead with a swastika tattoo on his face."

"Maybe."

"I met him in prison a few years back. He did a stretch for attempted murder. He's been staying with me since he got out. We're knocking over a pot dispensary by the highway called Papa Greens. It's easy money, but we need a third."

"Why me?"

"Because I trust you, and because you owe me."

"I don't owe you shit."

Scary used to buy heroin from Smoky Dave. He wasn't the nicest of guys. He'd short her and beat her when she came up short with his money. Smoky Dave's sister died of an overdose. It was rumored he was angry because she was stealing from him, so he spiked her hit. Scary avoided Smoky Dave when she got a better dealer, but he always claimed she still owed him when their paths crossed.

▼▼▼

Smoky Dave placed the barrel of the shotgun against the older woman's forehead as Screw smashed open the register, and emptied the cash into a black trash bag.

"Get them sweet nugs too," Smoky Dave said.

"Fucking stoner," Screw said, knocking dozens of small black plastic containers filled with various strains of marijuana into the bag.

"Bob Marley blunts tonight," Smoky Dave said just before the blast.

Smoky Dave dropped his weapon, and crumpled to the floor. Propped on his elbows in the doorway, the security guard fired again, grazing Scary's shoulder. Screw ducked behind the counter, and squeezed multiple rounds into the big man's face.

"Smoky Dave? You okay?" Screw asked, removing his ski mask. "Shit. Come on Scary. Let's dust these fucks and bounce."

Scary pointed the .45 at Screw.

"Fuck is wrong with you? Grab the money and let's dip. I'll take care of the witnesses."

"You used to beat up punkers with a baseball bat," Scary said. "A day doesn't go by that I don't dream of killing you."

"You were that kid's girl," Screw said in a moment of recognition. "The last twenty years haven't been kind to you."

"Rot in hell," Scary said, but Screw pulled the trigger first, shooting Scary in the gut, knocking her back against a shelf, and toppling dozens of hash-filled containers onto the floor.

▼▼▼

"I have something for you," Eddie said, handing Cary the aluminum tab he'd torn from a Coke can. "A talisman loaded with juju that will protect you from assholes."

"Why Mister Edward Jordan Green. I'll keep it always," Carry said in a phony southern accent, and squeezed his hand as they entered the Vet's hall.

Carry and Eddie bounced around the dance floor, bumping people in the mosh pit as their friends' band sped through three chord riffs. Near the end of the set, the musicians brought Eddie onto the stage, and started chanting, 'Eddie. Eddie Spaghetti. His meatballs are ready,' until everybody in the packed hall repeated the words. Eddie dove off the stage as the band tore into "The Eddie Spaghetti Song." After the show, Eddie kissed Carry on the sidewalk. Car brakes squealed, and punkers scattered as a gang of skinheads hopped out of the back of a pickup truck.

Eddie never saw his assailant swinging the baseball bat at the back of his cranium, but Carry did. She saw the hate in the man's eyes, and the swastika tattoo on his cheek. Eddie went down, and his skull bounced on the concrete like a basketball. His eyes rolled into the back of his head, and he bit his tongue. No matter how much heroin or meth Scary put into her veins in the coming years, she couldn't lose the image of Eddie convulsing on the ground.

▼▼▼

Screw placed the Glock to Scary's head, and pulled the trigger, but the chamber was empty. Scary's shot shattered Screw's jaw, and he collapsed into a corner, hissing blood. The hostages squirmed against the wall like sizzling sausage, frying in the fear of death. Scary felt warmth leaking from her side as she approached the wounded skinhead.

"Eddie. Eddie Spaghetti," she said, and replaced the swastika on Screw's cheek with a bullet hole. "His meatballs are ready."

The high-pitched whine of sirens approached as the hostages fled the dispensary's carnage. Scary sat on the blood-soaked floor, clutching the aluminum tab. Soon, there would be hell to pay, but Scary didn't care. She was protected.

The River never Tells

I was passing through town when I met a woman at Bronco's Bar and Grill. Janet wasn't the prettiest filly in the stable, but looks aren't everything. What she lacked in the beauty department, she made up for with an understanding ear and an ample bosom. By the third beer, I showed her the scar on my neck. By the fourth beer, she invited me to her place.

Janet lived by the river. There was something magical about that waterway. I didn't know what it was yet, but I felt fated to that tributary. Janet had a six-year-old son named Jimmy. That was weird. He was a little guy with red hair, and fully devoted to superheroes and Frosted Flakes. He ignored me, giving a batman movie his undivided attention, which was convenient on account of what Janet and I were about to do in her bedroom.

This was a good deal. I wanted to stay. Janet was onboard, but said I had to pull my own weight. She'd had several freeloading men in the past, and wasn't interested in supporting another deadbeat. I asked around town about work, and it wasn't long before I was told to try the sawmill up the hill.

I hitched a ride early one morning, but nobody was there. I wandered around the woodpiles, and looked

65

down a steep and misty ravine beyond the back of the lumberyard. A car approached, so I returned to the parking lot. A small truck passed, carrying three men. They parked, leaned against the side of the pickup, and scowled at me while spitting tobacco.

I was about to scratch this job opportunity when another truck pulled into the parking lot. A massive man oozed out of the cab, and heaved my way.

"Morning," he said. "What's your business?"

"Heard there might be work."

"You staying somewhere? Ain't camping out?"

"I got a roof overhead."

"Them's the magic words. We pay the minimum. You ever worked in a mill, used a saw?

"No."

"Perfect, we're looking for somebody to pile lumber. How's your back?"

"Fine," I said, and stood up straight.

"Welcome aboard," he said, but didn't shake my hand. "My name's Big Henry. You'll like it just fine around here."

"My name's Jake. Will they like me just fine around here?" I asked, shifting my eyes toward the three men, staring at me across the parking lot.

"That's Karl, Jerry, and Kemp. Don't worry. They're looking at you funny because they think you're homeless. The bums camping in the gorge behind the stacks steal our wood. The boys are getting mighty tired of it."

I set to work hauling lumber from the mill to the yard. Most of the other workers were friendly, and when Karl, Jerry and Kemp learned I held residency, my presence was tolerated. I wouldn't say we were peachy-keen or anything, but they didn't look like they wanted to kill me anymore.

I didn't have gloves, and my hands blistered. I was sore from head to toe, and dog-tired by the end of my shift. When I got to Janet's, the pain dissipated into her smile and her low-cut blouse. I sat on the back porch in contemplation, watching the water, and wondering why I felt so content. The reason eluded me, but as I stared into that hypnotic current, it hit me: with Janet, I was no longer following in my father's shadow. With Janet, I was my own man. Jimmy came out back, and disrupted my thoughts. He wanted to play superheroes, so I became the Incredible Hulk, and although my hands and back ached, I lifted him by the ankles, and swung him back and forth as he giggled with glee.

Jimmy gave me the lowdown on Bruce Wayne at the dinner table while Janet served hamburgers. I felt like I could have eaten a half-dozen, but I stopped after three when Janet gave me a look of amazement.

"I've never seen somebody wolf down so many hamburgers so fast," she said.

After Janet tucked Jimmy into bed, we smoked a joint and watched TV before hitting the sack. For the next several weeks, Janet would wake me on her way out the door with Jimmy. I'd pour a bowl of Frosted Flakes, make a pot of coffee, mourn my aching limbs and then thumb a ride up to the sawmill.

"That's the second pallet this week," Karl said. "They're building a city down there."

"They cut a hole in the fence," Jerry said. "That's how they steal lumber."

"Well boys, we need to mend that fence, pronto," Karl said with his thumbs sticking through his belt loops. "And we need to nip this situation in the bud. Once a pony gets a lump of sugar, he keeps on coming back for more."

"What do you propose?" Kemp asked.

"We have ourselves a problem for sure," Karl said. "But it's nothing a cold brew can't solve."

"Okay, everybody," Big Henry said, coming out of his office. "Get to work."

At lunchtime, we sat out back at picnic benches. Most guys ate sandwiches, but I never packed a lunch. Karl sat down, placed a six-pack of Budweiser on the table, and removed a beer. Jerry and Kemp each grabbed one. The guy next to me looked like he wanted to, but thought better of it, and left the table. Two other guys cautiously grabbed bottles. I was the last person, so I grabbed the last beer. We all cracked them and clinked necks. I took a sip, but noticed everybody chugging, so I did the same.

"Bring a hammer or a crowbar tomorrow an hour before work, agreed?" Karl asked.

"Agreed," they all said.

After lunch, Karl lent me gloves. I was worried I'd be unprepared for tomorrow's task, so I confided in him that I didn't have the required tools. He glared at me like we were back in the parking lot my first day, and then he laughed.

"Not to worry," he said. "I've got you covered."

I sat on Janet's back porch, drinking a beer and watching the river at sunset. I was worn out and hungry as hell. The routine was growing thin. A shadow stretched across my mind, and I wondered, is this really what I want? To be a broke roustabout, chained to a woman and child, or would it be better to be like Old Man River, and just keep rolling along? It'd be a damn sight easier. I could just wade out into the water, forget about the backbreaking work at the sawmill, forget about Janet and Jimmy, and float away. Several mosquitos bit me on the neck and face, so I went inside. I turned on the game, and Jimmy threw a temper tantrum. Janet promised him a Spiderman movie if he quieted down. I promised him an ass whooping if he didn't.

"Turn off the game, and put the Spiderman movie on, and don't you ever threaten him again," Janet said.

"Fine," I said, putting on the DVD. "He wants to watch a guy prancing around in colorful tights instead of football, who am I to judge?"

"Football's full of guys prancing around in colorful tights," Janet said.

"Enjoy your movie," I said to Jimmy. "Your mom and I'll be in the back, having private time."

"Not tonight, Jake," she said.

"Come on," I told her, but she wasn't interested. "Fine, I'll watch this shit with the kid. Any beer in the fridge?"

"What did you just say?"

"You cooking anymore hamburgers?" I asked.

"You can get out," she yelled. "And don't come back if you're going to disrespect my family. You hear me fucker?"

I spent the evening wandering along the river, thinking to hell with this town, this job and this woman. I didn't need any of it. In the morning, I'd follow the river to somewhere else.

I found a sandy spot and lay down.

The cool dark water rushed by and the stars speckled the evening sky. My troubles faded into the river's tranquility, and I felt light as air. A splashing sound nearby interrupted my momentary contentment. I looked out over the black current, but saw only moving water. I heard another splashing sound that caused me to sit up, and train my eyes into the darkness. Something large and sinister with glowing yellow eyes crawled out of the river under the night's shadows. Its long razor-sharp jaws grabbed me by the neck, and dragged me into the water. I kicked and punched and flailed, but to no avail.

As the creature held me under, crushing my windpipe, I saw my father's face.

I woke in a cold sweat. It was first light, and I was still on the sandy bank. My neck was stiff, but intact. I was groggy, but made my way to the highway, and caught a ride up to the mill. My stomach growled. I was haggard and irritable from sleeping on the ground.

"About time you showed," Karl said, handing me a crowbar. "We was about to leave your ass. Let's get a move on."

We walked through the stacks in the back of the lumberyard. At the rear fence, we came to a locked gate.

"Over there's the hole they made," Jerry said, producing a key from his pocket.

A steep dirt trail wound down through thick shrubs and thorny blackberry vines. The sun glowed through the treetops. I hadn't understood what the job entailed until we left the yard for the forest. I thought this was on the up and up, but as we entered the brush, the gravity of the situation hit me.

The forest was dense, and the trail grew narrow. I thought about my father and how he had walked out on us so many years ago. I took a deep breath, and thought about Janet and Jimmy. I wished I were in bed with Janet, or pouring a bowl of Frosted Flakes for Jimmy instead of descending into the mist with Karl and the boys.

We hit the canyon floor and came to a stream. Around a bend, we got our first glimpse of the homeless camp. Several shacks built from pillaged lumber leaned against large knotty pines on the far shore.

We crossed the stream on dry rocks. As we landed on the far strand, a man stuck his head out of the closest shanty.

"Goddamn thief," Karl shouted, raising his hammer.

The man hollered, and fled into the bush. A din erupted as the occupants of the other shacks realized the danger and scrambled into the safety of the woods.

"Knock down these rat's nests," Karl said.

"What's the point?" Jerry asked. "They'll just rebuild them."

"Pile everything on the shore. The lumber, all their garbage, everything," Karl said. "We're having a bonfire, boys."

"Wish we'd got our hands on those sons of bitches," Jerry said as we dismantled the hovels, and piled their belongings next to the stream.

Mostly cardboard and blankets lined the floors, but there were also stoves and clothing. I also found some stuffed animals and children's books. We heaped it on the shore, and Kemp lit a fire.

"Hey," Jerry yelled when he entered the last shack. "We got one. He's piss drunk."

"Bring him over here," Karl said.

They dragged the guy by his ankles to the bonfire.

"You stealing our wood, boy?" Karl asked.

The man's head swayed on his neck. He was dirty and in need of a shave and a haircut. Like me, the poor fellow was late in comprehending his predicament. Karl slugged him in the gut. He gave out a bellowing yowl of pain mixed with fear. The others fell on the inebriated guy, cursing and working him over with angry fists.

I stood back, watching them beat the transient. That could have been me: some poor bastard, down-and-out, and in the wrong place at the wrong time.

"Come on," Karl yelled. "Don't just stand there."

"Yeah, you fucking idiot," Jerry yelled. "We're all doing this."

I hesitated for a moment, and then walked over to the luckless man and clocked him in the head with my crowbar. I'll never forget that hollow sound.

"Jesus Christ," Karl said. "What did you do that for? I wanted to rough him up. Teach him a lesson, not bash in his brains."

"Hey guys," Kemp said. "The fire."

"Holy shit," Karl said. "It's catching the brush."

"Let's go," Jerry said.

We crossed back over the stream. Sweat poured down my face as we hustled up the narrow trail to the fence at the back of the lumberyard. Jerry's hand trembled as he locked the gate behind us.

"What the hell you boys doing?" Big Henry asked.

"We was fixing that hole in the fence when we saw the fire," Karl said.

Henry frowned, but didn't ask any more questions. He told us to evacuate the area. Dark smoke clouds rose from beneath us into the sky. It wasn't long before sirens approached.

I went straight to Janet's and apologized for last night's behavior. I wanted to make it up by taking her and Jimmy out to eat. Janet liked that idea. She dressed pretty, slicked down Jimmy's hair, and we went to Bronco's.

For dinner, I had a double cheeseburger with bacon and a dark beer. Janet had the fish and chips and a glass of white wine. Jimmy had the macaroni and cheese with bacon and a root beer. It was a nice meal, but we sat near the television in the bar. Everybody around us watched the news and talked about the fire.

"Those bums started it," the bartender said. "A couple of firefighters almost lost their lives. Almost lost the sawmill."

"A homeless guy burned to death," our waitress said.

"Good," a man at the bar said. "Serves his freeloading ass right."

We went back to Janet's. I tucked Jimmy into bed, and read him a Curious George story. Once he fell asleep, I went into the living room and cuddled with Janet.

After a few days, the mill reopened. None of the guys would talk to me. Karl asked for his gloves back, but that was it. They treated me like a ghost, like a wood piling specter. Before the weekend, a detective arrived.

"Where were you when the fire started?"

His name was Detective Banks. He was old and wrinkled with a purple nose, but he had a severe stare that worried me.

"I just arrived when I saw the smoke," I said.

"Can others attest to that?" He asked.

"Yes," I said.

I finished my shift at the mill, but I couldn't catch a ride so I walked. As the sun went down behind heavy cloud cover, the shadows from the trees grew into the road, and enveloped me in growing darkness. With each step, my mood blackened. There had better be some hot food waiting for me on the table, I thought, and Jimmy had better be on his best behavior. I wasn't going to put up with his shit tonight. As I made my way down the road, I had the strange sensation that something was following me. I peered into the gloom beyond the edge of the trees.

I stepped off the side of the road into the duff. A chill wind cut through me. In the shadows, a set of yellow eyes appeared, staring at me from within the forest. I took another step toward the trees as a drop of rain hit my forehead. I looked up at the sky. Storm clouds ran overhead like the river's current. Stepping back onto the road, I quickened my pace.

I was soaked by the time I reached Janet's front door. Detective Banks stood in the living room. Janet sat on the couch. Jimmy was on her lap. Tears flowed from her eyes. The detective squinted at me. My pulse quickened, and my face reddened, and the scar on my neck burned. I clenched my teeth and fists as dread filled my chest.

"It's Sean," Janet said.

"Who?" I asked.

"Jimmy's dad," she said.

"What about him?"

"He's dead," she sobbed.

"They identified him as the victim of the fire," Detective Banks said. "We suspect he was high, and trying to cook another dose when he passed out and started the blaze."

I breathed a sigh of relief, releasing the bad thoughts inside. I tried to ease Janet and Jimmy's grief. I did the dishes, swept the floor, and made hamburgers. They didn't turn out good like Janet's, but they were edible. I put on Spiderman, and let Jimmy tell me about Peter Parker. After he went to bed, I stayed up consoling Janet.

The next morning after making breakfast for Janet and Jimmy, I thumbed it up to the sawmill. The rain had stopped in the night, and the ground was wet and fresh smelling. My ride let me off in the back of the parking lot. I walked toward the main building as Karl's truck passed me.

"Good morning," I said as I reached the front of the parking lot.

They leaned against the automobile, spitting tobacco.

"For some," Karl said, wiping spit from his chin. "For others, not so much."

"I'd hate to be you, right now," Jerry said. "In a world of shit."

"What are you saying?" I asked.

"What you done to that homeless guy," Kemp said. "I wouldn't want to be wearing your shoes."

"Hold on a second," I said, looking at my sneakers. "We're all to blame for what happened."

"Not according to us," Kemp said.

"Who started the fire?" I asked.

"Depends," Karl said.

"On?"

"Payday."

"I smell where you're stepping," I said.

"Knew you would," Karl said.

I went about piling lumber. At the end of my shift, Big Henry paid me in cash. It wasn't much, but it was enough to show Janet that I could pull my own weight. I tried to hitch it down the hill, but I couldn't catch a ride, so I walked.

"Jake, where you been?" Karl asked, pulling alongside me. "Thought we were squaring up."

"That's right. I almost forgot," I said, and kept walking. "I tell you what. Now's not a good time. What say we square up later?"

"Hop in the back of the pickup, and we'll discuss," Karl said, leveling a handgun at me.

"All right," I said, and climbed in the bed of the truck.

Karl turned onto a bumpy dirt road. We went down the gnarled path for several miles. Scanning the bed for a weapon, I saw only old beer cans, empty bullet shells and fast-food wrappers until I found a tire iron under a ripped-up tarp.

The sun ducked beneath a row of pine as Karl pulled over.

"Give me your money," Karl said, pointing the gun at my chest.

"You'll have pissed your pants when we get done with you," Jerry said.

"Doesn't seem like a square deal," I said. "Giving you my money, and getting the piss beat out of me."

"Sure, it does," Karl said.

"How do you figure?" I asked.

"The money buys our silence. The beating lets you know that you should move on."

"What if I keep my money, and beat the shit out of you instead?" I asked.

They laughed, closing in around me. I picked up the tire iron, and flung it at Karl. Diving out of the truck, I tackled Jerry, and knocked him to the ground. He instantly went limp, so I got to my feet, and went for Karl, but he was already in the truck, turning over the engine. He sped off as Kemp tried to open the passenger side door, but was dragged to the ground, and flipped onto his head.

I went for the tire iron, but noticed the gun beside it. Kemp picked himself up out of the road. He was covered in mud, and blood dripped out of his ear. He limped over to Jerry.

"What was the play?" I asked.

Neither man said anything, so I cocked back the hammer, and repeated myself.

"Take your dough. Leave you for dead," Jerry whispered with his eyes closed.

"What if instead," I asked. "I take your dough, and leave you for dead?"

Kemp reached into his pocket, and tossed me his money. I noticed a dark pool forming around Jerry's head. When I knocked him to the ground, he must have cracked his skull on a rock.

"You sure the second part of your plan was to leave me for dead?" I asked. "Sure it wasn't to leave me dead?"

"Don't matter," Jerry whispered. "Karl's heading straight to the police to tell them what you did."

"What I did? What we all did. You're both as guilty as me. Karl too. I never wanted to hurt anybody."

"That's your story," Jerry said in a low tone. "I don't remember it that way."

"How do you remember it?"

"You smashing that guy's head in with a crowbar."

"Is that how you remember it too, Kemp?" I asked. "Do you remember starting the fire?"

"I can't remember nothing," he said.

"But back in town, your memory returns, right?"

"Don't matter the way I feel right now," he said, touching his bloody ear.

"Then let's have the truth," I said.

"Take your dough. Make it so nobody finds your body," he said.

I thought about pulling the trigger, but as much as I wanted to, I couldn't do it.

I left Jerry and Kemp on the side of the road and walked at a quick clip. I wished Karl hadn't gotten away. Soon he'd tell the police I murdered Jimmy's dad and set the fire. It was only a matter of time before Janet found out what they were accusing me of, and for that, she'd never forgive me. Time would have bought an engagement ring, a wedding, and a proper upbringing for Jimmy, but now time was the enemy.

I ditched the gun, and walked for hours in the dark until I came to the main road. I heard an automobile approaching, so I hid behind a large tree. A sheriff's truck drove by. I stayed put, and another passed.

In a short time, the sheriffs would find Jerry and Kemp, and they'd corroborate Karl's story. I was a wanted man. Heading to Janet's on the main road was no longer an option, so I started up the hill along the side of the road, skirting the edge of the forest.

The parking lot at the sawmill was empty except for a truck near the front. I walked around back through the stacks, and was just about to reach the fence when somebody lurched in front of me with a shotgun.

"Hold up, Jake," Big Henry said. "Police radio says you're wanted in connection with arson and homicide."

"I didn't do it," I said.

"That might be so, but you're staying put until the cops arrive," he said.

"I can't," I said, and ducked behind a stack of lumber.

I reached the back gate, but it was locked, so I felt my way down the side until I came to the hole in the fence. As I crawled through, buckshot ripped into my thigh. I fell onto the other side as another blast stung my shoulder, neck and face. I tumbled down the ravine and over an embankment. Fortunately, a tangle of vines and reeds broke my fall. I thrashed around, and when my shoes touched the ground, they filled with water.

I limped downstream. With every step the current grew deeper and stronger. I waded in the cold water until the stream became a river, and I swam with my head bobbing out of the runnel.

The river's gradient steepened, and I struggled to stay afloat in the turbulent white water. The rapids pushed me through several narrow crevasses, and over submerged boulders until I was caught in a powerful eddy, and an undercurrent pinned me beneath the water. After a short time, my struggles for oxygen evaporated into peaceful blackness. I thought about Janet as my limbs relaxed. Just before I lost consciousness, the undertow relented, and I rose to the surface, gasping and choking.

The river calmed as the waterway widened. Stars shone bright overhead, and every so often a meteor flashed across the sky. I was cold and tired as I reached my destination and swam to shore. My body shivered as I staggered to my feet. Tiny blood rivulets trickled down my face, arms and legs, mingling with my wet garments.

I threw myself into the backdoor, and it burst open.

"Don't move. Stay where you are," Detective Banks shouted.

I stumbled through the kitchen, and barreled into the living room as he opened fire. It felt like a mule kicked me in the chest, and I fell backwards. The detective stood over me, pointing his weapon. I closed my eyes, and was about to quit when I heard screams coming from the bedroom.

"I said don't move," Detective Banks ordered as I turned onto my belly, dragging myself through the hall.

He fired several shots into my back, but I was able to reach the knob and open the door.

Janet huddled in the corner, holding Jimmy. I took a deep and labored breath.

I made it.

I was home.

Flower Man

With a 6 pack under his tattooed arm, Cash steps into the crosswalk. Tires squeal and a pickup skids over the white line. Crashing over the hood, Cash bounces off the front window. He lands on his head in the middle of the street. Beer cans roll on the asphalt, hissing foamy little lager geysers.

"Flower Man, this the guy?" A mountain of a man asks the driver as he hops out the passenger-side of the truck.

"You know it is, Fat Ass," the silver ponytailed driver says, wearing a sunflower patterned shirt.

"How do I know?" Fat Ass asks with a distant look in his eye.

"It's fuckin' Cash. Used to be our boy, ripped off Capo. You know him," Flower Man says.

"Just asking," Fat Ass says, taking out his pistol.

Cash reaches for his .38, but the gun is not in his coat pocket. In the gutter, just out of arm's reach, he spies his weapon. As a bullet ricochets on the concrete near his head, Cash rolls. In a single motion, he grabs his pistol and pulls the trigger three times. The big man collapses in a massive heap, his head a gory mess.

Climbing to his feet, Cash recovers his wallet, phone, and an intact can of beer with one hand. He points the gun in his other hand at the truck. Flower Man stomps the gas. Cash fires three rounds into the cab. The vehicle swerves hard left into oncoming traffic, and then hard right, colliding head on with a lamppost.

Cash touches the swelling around the back of his head as he enters the apartment's courtyard. Derelict cars, used diapers and a rusty shopping cart litter the weedy lawn. On the landing, Cash reaches into his pocket, but finds no key. He searches his other pocket, but locates only lint. With a sigh, he sets his beer on the welcome mat.

His head throbs as he skinnies onto the ledge, reaching for the half open second floor window. Cash pops out the screen, and pulls himself through the frame onto the kitchen table. Movement from the front room has his finger on the gun's trigger.

"What the hell, Cash," Eva says, hunching in fear.

"Thought you were somebody else. I lost my key, so I came through the window."

"Try knocking next time. What do you mean somebody else?" She asks, smoothing down her short black bangs.

"I just ran into Flower Man, or rather, he ran into me with his truck in the crosswalk."

"You okay? Your hair's a mess and your jeans and jacket are torn."

"He had that big son of a bitch, Fat Ass, with him," Cash says, running his fingers through his greasy pompadour.

"What happened?" Eva asks, sitting at the table, and putting on her wing-tipped glasses.

"I don't care how fat your ass is. Three up top, and you plop. His head cracked like an egg on the curb, and his brains slid into the gutter."

"They couldn't have been very big brains. Fat Ass was the dumbest shit in the pit. Did you do Flower Man too?" Eva asks, putting on red lipstick.

"I think so."

"Is he dead or not?"

"I don't know. I squeezed off every last shot into his truck, and he crashed into a lamppost."

Somebody pounds on the front door. Looking through the murky peephole, Cash draws his gun.

"Who is it?" Eva asks as Cash opens the door.

"What a dump," Big Ray says, drinking the beer Cash left on the porch. "What's wrong with your hair? You need some Pomade?"

"You're not staying with us," Eva says as Big Ray belches, rattling the toothpick in the gap between his front teeth.

"Anymore beer?"

"You got the first and last one," Cash says, and describes to Big Ray his encounter with Flower Man and Fat Ass, and the loss of five of his six beers.

"You got some real heat coming down on you," Big Ray says, removing a flask from his pocket, and taking a long pull. "Robbing Capo has that effect. He wants his drug money back, and he wants to staple your balls to your tongue."

"Charming," Eva says.

"No matter what two-fuck, fogged out beach haunt you hide in, they'll find you. Flower Man did, so did I," Big Ray says, slicking back his hair with his hand. "Capo's on your ass, and he's about the nuttiest hitter that ever was. How much you pilfer anyway?"

"I didn't steal shit," Cash says. "I'm not stupid enough to rob Capo."

"That's not what Capo thinks," Big Ray says, lighting a cigarette, and taking a long drag. "Come on. Don't hold out on me."

"I got nothing to let you borrow if that's what you think. Besides, you still owe me five hundred."

"Not borrow. Earn," Big Ray says, plopping down on the couch, and popping a few pills. "You have the weight of a criminal organization stepping on your dick. Flower Man and Fat Ass are just the tip of the toe. You need protection."

"We aren't hiring you as our bodyguard, Big Ray," Eva says, lighting a cigarette. "Get your ass up. You ain't staying here."

The fire alarm wakes Cash and Eva in the middle of the night. Cash stumbles into the living room, and finds the rug on fire. Cash flips the rug, and stamps out the flames. Upon investigation into the source of the fire, Cash quickly deduces that Big Ray zonked out on the couch with a lit cigarette in his hand. The embers fell onto the rug, and ignited the fire. Even now through the horridness of the wailing alarm, Big Ray sleeps. Cash thinks about slugging the fathead in his snoring face, but instead he decides to deal with the situation in daylight. He returns to the bedroom when the alarm stops screaming.

In the morning, Eva steps into the kitchen to brew coffee, wearing a red-checkered dress. Cash slumps into the kitchen behind her, rubbing his swollen head.

"Goddamn, Big Ray," Cash says with a yawn. "Wake your ass up, and get out. You almost burned down this shithole. Dumb bastard thinks I robbed Capo. Ray, wake your ass up. Big Ray. Ray?"

"Cash?" Eva asks, "Where did these flowers come from?"

Cash sees a bouquet of daisies on the kitchen counter, and then notices Ray's slit throat.

"Flower Man. When he hit me with the truck, my belongings scattered every which way. I gathered my gun, wallet, phone and a beer, but when I returned home, I didn't have my key. I left it on the street. I thought I killed Flower Man, but instead, he found my key, and followed me home. He let himself in in the early morning hours, killed Big Ray, and left flowers as his calling card. We would have been pushing up daisies too, had the fire alarm not scared off our would-be assassin."

"Grab the keys," Eva says. "We should have left yesterday."

Cash and Eva exit the apartment, and climb into her 61' Impala. Flower Man appears behind them with a pistol in his hand. He unloads his weapon into the back of the car as Cash stomps the gas in reverse. Flower Man tumbles onto the hood. A smear of blood sticks to the windshield. Cash punches the car forward, and stomps the brake, causing Flower Man to roll off the hood. The old man with the ponytail and floral shirt kneels on the asphalt. Blood pours out his mouth.

"This is how you pull off a hit-and-run, asshole," Cash says, lighting a cigarette.

Two jarring thumps later, and Flower Man is just a piece of twisted refuse, fading in the rearview mirror. Out on the highway, Cash uses the windshield wipers to clear the blood from the glass.

"Got me in the leg. Hurts like hell. Won't stop bleeding."

"I know a vet named Hal. He'll fix you right up on the hush."

"Cash?"

"Yeah?"

"I hid the money I stole from Capo in my sister's attic. She doesn't know it's there. I want you to take half, and give her the other half."

"Hal is going to fix you right up." Cash says, obliterating the speed limit.

After a few minutes of silence, Cash lights a cigarette and looks at Eva. He pulls over, opens the passenger-side door, and lets her lifeless body slump into the dirt. In the rearview mirror, Eva's red-checkered dress flutters in the wind, dissipating in the distance. A few miles later, he finds a southbound onramp.

If Cash remembers correctly, Eva's sister lives in Los Angeles.

The Exterminator

I take a long swig of vodka as I park the truck. I take another pull from the bottle, sling my sprayer over my shoulder, and walk up the red brick path to a white stucco mansion.

A woman answers the door, and an electric bolt of lust shocks my alcohol-logged heart. Under a red blanket draped around her shoulders, a black bikini hangs on for dear life. Long thick waves of brunette hair partially obscure her face. She reveals a spider tattoo on her wrist as she sets down a cocktail on the floor and lights a cigarette.

"You made an appointment with Carson Pest Control," I say. "I'm Randy."

"I'm Sam," she says, leading me into a newly remodeled kitchen.

"You got ants."

"You must be an entomologist," she says, taking a drag from her cigarette, and sweeping back her thick hair, revealing a particularly nasty black eye.

"How'd you get that?"

"My husband's a mean drunk."

"What a piece of shit. That crap gets me heated."

"You getting heated, Randy?" She asks, stepping toward me. "My husband is in the tech industry. Writes code for a fast-food delivery app. You want a vodka tonic?"

She leads me out back to a large kidney shaped pool with a fully stocked cabana. I trounce the alcoholic beverage she hands me as she sheds her red blanket onto an Adirondack chair, and dives into the shimmering water. When she emerges from the drink, she's topless.

"I'm bored," she says, brushing against my shoulder. She pours another vodka tonic, and takes a long sip. "Tell me a joke."

"Nah, I'm fresh out of wise cracks," I say, pulling her wet body into mine, and kissing her hard on the mouth.

Post coitus, Sam lays naked in the pool on a swan shaped flotation device, smoking a cigarette while I pour another drink at the cabana.

"I want you to kill my husband."

"I only kill bugs."

"That's what he is," she says. "A vile insect that needs to be eradicated."

"I'll pass," I say. "But thanks for considering me for the job."

I lift my sprayer, and head for the ant superhighway in the kitchen. A man in his late twenties opens the front door. He's bearded with long hair pulled back into a man bun. He wears skinny black jeans, a red-checkered flannel, and leather sandals as he saunters into the kitchen to make a drink.

"Follow me," he commands.

"Randy," I say, holding out my hand. "Carson Pest Control."

He leaves me hanging as we climb a large staircase, and walk through a doorway.

"Spray in here," he says, and walks away, sipping his drink.

As I fumigate, Sam slips into the room, sliding her body against mine.

"You met Nathan," she says. "He's a douche, right?"

"I wouldn't say we met."

"He's worth a fortune, you know."

"Assholes always are, but that ain't cause to kill 'em."

"You murder things all day," she says lighting a cigarette. "That's your job."

"No thanks, Sam."

After work, I drive to the liquor store, buy a cheap handle of vodka, and head out to the bluff, overlooking the city.

My ex-wife calls me a deadbeat, and won't let me see my boy. He's got a heart condition.

My bones ache from past fractures–a sure sign of rain. Dark rolling clouds further confirm my weather prediction. As the sun sets beyond the bluff, the lights from the city below blur in waving sheets of falling water.

As I take a rip from the bottle, somebody taps on the glass.

"Evening sir," a police officer says as I roll down the window. "Can I see your driver's license and registration?"

"Can you repeat that?" I ask.

"Step out of the car, sir."

"He reeks of booze," a second officer says.

"What are you doing here?" The first officer asks.

"Astrology," I say.

"Huh?" the second officer asks.

"I'm star gazing, genius."

"You want to see stars?" The first cop asks just before the baton strikes my knee. "You come to the right place."

I go down in the mud, and nightsticks play paradiddles on my head until the stars go out.

I wake up feeling like a busted two-by-four in a strange bed that also feels like a busted two-by-four.

"Stay down," a doctor says, and his hand presses against my forehead. "Some hooker found you laying in a puddle of blood out in the rain. She thought you were dead."

"I wish I were."

"There's still time. I looked over your charts. Can I be candid, Randal? Your liver is about to shit the bed. You've been a binge drinker for most of your adult life. You won't last long if you keep consuming alcohol at this rate."

They release me from the hospital on the day I am scheduled for a follow up appointment at Sam and Nathan's house. I arrive at the track mansion with a bottle of vodka between my legs. I kill the drink, and grab my sprayer. Blasting a steady stream of insect death up the walkway, I make my way into the backyard. Sam is poolside, draped in her red blanket, and sucking down a vodka tonic. She glances at me with a new black eye on the other side of her face, and then she returns to some fashion magazine. Nathan comes out to the cabana and makes himself a drink.

"Babe, I'm heading downtown. I've got some business I need to attend to," he says, and finishes his drink.

"Bye-bye," Sam says, lighting a cigarette. "Make sure to tell that little whore, I say hello."

"The bugs are back," Nathan says to me. "I was talking to a friend and he says you have to get under the house and destroy the nests. I don't want to tell you how to do your job, but I don't want to pay you for nothing, either."

"He wants you under the house like a bug," Sam says when her husband leaves.

"I want half of what he's worth."

"Half?" she asks, lighting a cigarette. "That's a terrible deal."

"I won't kill a man for peanuts," I say. "My son has a bad ticker. Can you believe it? And my ex, she won't let me see the little guy. Doctors think my liver is about to go belly up too. I got to help my boy while I can."

"Nathan'll come home tonight, beat me and drink himself blackout drunk as he does every night. When he's passed out, I'll text you. Do you like this blanket?"

"Sure," I say and take a sip from her vodka tonic. "I like you a lot without it too."

"It was my mother's. Do you understand? She gave it to me. It's mine. Everything else is his, but not this blanket."

"Like I said," I say, sliding the red blanket from her shoulders and dropping it onto the Adirondack chair. "I like you better without it."

Later that night, I drink vodka in my truck. I try not to think about Nathan, and how I want to back out of this whole rotten mess.

"He's out by the pool," she whispers when I return.

"Half, right?"

Sprawled out on an Adirondack chair, Nathan's eyes are shut and vomit smears his beard. He snores loudly as I place a trash bag over his head, and wrap duct tape around his neck. His hands instinctively clutch at the sheet of thick plastic. I tag him hard in the gut, and he collapses on the concrete next to the pool. Sam opens the garage door, and I back my work truck up the driveway. A faint moan emanates from the plastic bag as I drag Nathan to my vehicle.

On the highway, nobody's around. My work truck climbs steep roads through dark woods. A turnout appears through massive silhouetted trees. I pull off at the vista point, and kill the headlights as a car rounds the bend. It's headlights flash across my work truck before passing back into the darkness.

I take a swig of vodka, and let down the tailgate. Scooping Nathan under my arm, I drag him toward the edge of the cliff. He moans something unintelligible under the trash bag. I give Nathan another gut shot. He doubles over, and I kick him square in the ass.

In my truck, I crack another bottle. The vodka slides down my throat as I realize I forgot to remove the trash bag from Nathan's head.

A few days later, and I still have not heard from Sam, so I get a belly full of vodka, and I drive my work truck to her place. I spray along the walkway to make it look like I am there on a call.

"A hunter found Nathan impaled by a tree branch," Sam says when I enter the backyard. "They airlifted him to Stanford. It's all over the news."

"I need a drink," I say but before I can get to the vodka at the cabana, a voice startles us.

"Am I interrupting something?" A man says, approaching from behind.

"Who are you?" Sam asks, "I'm calling the cops."

"Hold your ponies," The man says, extending his hand for a shake. "You'd only be ringing me. Detective Banks. You must be Samantha Gray."

"Yes."

"Sorry to bug you ma'am," he says. "I need to ask you a few questions. I know this must be difficult."

"Yes."

"We will find the person who did this to Nathan, and when we do, I will personally see to it that their punishment goes far beyond the extent that the law can implement. I didn't catch your name," Detective Banks says to me.

"He's the exterminator," Sam says.

"You got a business card or something?" Detective Banks asks.

"Fresh out," I say, and walk around the side of the house, pretending to fumigate.

Detective Banks and Sam talk for a while before he finally leaves.

"What did he say?"

"He said Nathan is awake, and will soon be talking," she says, clutching her blanket. "You fucked up in record time."

"He doesn't know it's you," I say.

"They'll find out."

"I'll take the fall and keep your name out of it, Sam, but you got to do me a favor."

"In the master bedroom is a safe. The combination is written on the inside of the medicine cabinet's mirror in the bathroom. Take the cash and go."

I locate the combination, but it takes several tries to open the safe. It also takes time to count the thirty-grand inside. I'll just peel off a few hundred and get ripped like never before tonight, and tomorrow, I'll give my boy the money, and turn myself in.

Sam isn't in the backyard when I return, so I make a vodka tonic at the cabana. Dropping the full glass on the concrete, I run to the edge of the pool. Facedown in the water, Sam floats motionless, wrapped in her mother's red blanket.

Charlie Knuckles

Tommy wraps my hands in the back room as Fran enters to wish me luck.

"How goes, Ryker?" He asks, taking the cigar out of his mouth. "Ready to rip this clown's nuts off?"

"Yeah," I say.

"Good camp? Eat clean, cycle your PEDs, put in hard work?"

"Yeah."

"You go down in the second."

"Come on, Fran," Tommy says. "Jaxon's about to turkey."

"No surprises," Fran says, and spits on the ground. "Charlie Knuckles goes down in the second, and we all get paid. You got that little hotty at home, Sarah Sweets. I seen her wiggling ass on pole down Trinity's. You got to keep a honey like that happy. Happy takes money, not that nickel and dime shit you scrape on the amateur circuit."

"No surprises," I say.

Fran grabs his balls, farts and leaves the room.

Tommy smirks with a whistle sound escaping the gap between his front teeth. He puts in a lot of time helping me improve my game. Long after everybody else goes home, we drill various repetitions. Traps and trips, head kicks and combinations. Tommy puts in the extra time with me because he sees my potential.

"You broke Sprat's jaw, and strangled Edwards," he says. "One win away from a turkey, and this piece-of-shit flips the script."

"Don't think about it, Tommy. It's out our hands."

"All that sacrifice so fuck-o can make a bill. You won't get shit off this."

"When it's my time, Fran'll make it happen."

"The turkey makes it happen. A turkey means better billing, more money, better fights, the whole shebang. A loss don't do shit except make us hit reset. I'd hate for you to end up a shill journeyman for that dirtbag," Tommy says, and puts on the pads.

I'm stiff as I snap my first few combinations, but once I fire several kicks, my heart rate quickens, and the blood pumps through my chest.

As I walk out, Fran winks. Drunks pack the venue. A referee checks my gloves, smears Vaseline on my face, checks for a mouthpiece, and taps my junk to make sure I'm cupped. My adrenaline jacks as I enter the cage.

I'm fighting a Texan named Bull Johnson. Bull's also on a two-fight win streak, but everybody knows this bum doesn't stand a chance. He's just a scared little cow, and I'm the big bad hamburger factory. The safe money is on me. Fran knows this, so he tilts the scale.

Bull enters the cage, jumps around, and flexes his muscles, like I'm supposed to shit my pants. As the ring announcer introduces me as Jaxson "Charlie Knuckles" Ryker, I put up my hand: the universal sign to touch gloves. Bull nods in the affirmative. This is the only time in the fight it is okay to make contact with Charlie Knuckles: the intro fist bump. After that it's all brain swelling charley horses and nap inducing knuckle sandwiches.

"Protect yourself at all times," the referee barks, and the bell thuds. We move to the center of the cage. Just before we bump fists, Bull sucker punches me with a massive left haymaker in the eye. I wobble as he grabs a takedown, and dumps me on my head. Twinkling stars dance in my vision. The referee takes a close look.

I'm supposed to lose, but not like this.

I buck my hips, and explode into a scramble. In a flash, I return to my feet. Blood drips from my nose like a leaky tap, and my right eye swells shut. Bull throws a spinning heel kick, but I'm out of range. A superman punch grazes my shoulder.

Annoyed by his cheap shots and theatrics, I stick out a jab. The punch explodes on Bull's chin like a grenade. He stumbles about like a three-year-old on ice skates. I intentionally miss my next combination for fear of knocking him unconscious. Bull clenches me against the cage, and I allow him to hold on for dear life.

Fear fills Bull's eyes. He thinks I've flipped the script. The ten-second warning sounds. I throw a hard kick to the midsection. Bull drops to one knee, gasping as the bell ends the round.

"Fuck this chump," Tommy says in my corner. "He don't belong here. This guy belongs in a Disney princess dress, getting diddled by Mickey Mouse."

In the front row, I see Fran chewing uneasily on his stogie. I wink as the cut man jams a wad of cotton swabs up my nostrils.

Round two begins, and Bull throws sloppy looping overhands that I can dodge with my eyes closed, but for the sake of the flop, I plant my feet, and absorb the blows. Bull's punches have about as much pop as an open Pepsi left overnight in the fridge. He throws a head kick, connecting behind my ear. This is my cue. I should dive, but instead I fire the jab. It lands real estate on my opponent's tin chin, and Bull loses his upright privilege.

'Fuck it,' I think as he flops around senseless like a fish on land, and I drop a savage sledgehammer fist on Bull's slack jaw.

Tommy and my team go ballistic, rushing into the cage to celebrate. I should celebrate too. Charlie Knuckles' first turkey, but I don't because I'm fucked.

En route to my old beat-up pickup truck in the parking lot after the fight, the barrel of a gun pokes me in the ribs. Large men flank my sides, guiding me into a black limousine. I'm sandwiched between two brutes in the backseat while a little guy sits opposite, leveling a pistol at my chest.

"Congrats on your turkey," he says.

I tell them about Bull's glass jaw, but they just laugh.

At best I'm hoping for a tune up, but we've been driving for long enough to know I'm in for some serious middle of the desert bullshit. Eventually the limo pulls over along a dirt road. I don't go down without a fight. As I exit the vehicle, I bust a thug's jaw with my fist. He drops like a sack of shit, but before I get my hands on the next guy, the gun butt cracks my noggin, and I hit the sand, face first.

The upright goon takes up the spade.

"Fuck you doing?" Little Guy asks. "We don't dig."

"If we don't, who does? … oh," he says, throwing the shovel at me.

I stagger to my feet, and dig my own grave under the threat of death. I sob and plead for life, giving them a good chuckle.

"Turkey don't always mean thanksgiving," Little Guy says.

Broken Jaw gains his feet, holding the side of his pissed off face. He errors into my shovel range, and I give his fractured jaw a busted nose friend. Little Guy with the big gun rips one into the night sky before leveling the weapon at my chest.

"You okay?" He asks his downed and physically altered companion, but a sad whimper like a sick puppy is the only sound Broken Jaw musters. "Hurry up with that pit, kid. I ain't got all night."

Asshole couldn't be more wrong. He has all night, and the next and the next and the next. I'm the one deprived of sunrise.

The gun persuades me to continue my labor. When the pit is deep enough, Little Guy orders me in the fresh plot. I think about Sarah, her curves, the way she smiles, her nipples.

"On your stomach," Little Guy says.

I close my eyes, awaiting admittance into the void, but when the bang comes, my soul remains intact.

"Out you go," a voice says.

I climb from my grave, and see Broken Jaw has a bullet hole in his forehead to match his crushed nose. Fran with a gun, stands over the dead thug. Little Guy's tiny face reads disappointment.

"Do me a favor, Jaxon," Fran says, tossing me the shovel. "Bury this bum, would you?"

"What'd he do?" I ask.

"Got too far behind. Cheaper just to off him, and put it on you. A two birds with one stone kind of deal," Fran says, burps and spits in the sand. "We had a deal. You fucked that up. Now you have consequences."

"You leaving me out here?"

Fran climbs into the limo, and its glowing red taillights shrink in the distance as a pair of harsh white headlights approach. A jeep parks alongside the gravesite, and a sheriff with a big cowboy hat climbs out the cab, holding a shotgun.

"Evening," he says. "Or is it morning?"

"Whichever you prefer," I say, tossing the shovel on the ground, and hold up my hands under the dark desert sky.

"What you got there?" he asks, moving slowly around me to peer into the pit.

"Ain't mine," I say.

"You best be making sweet love to the ground, boy," he says, racking the gauge.

When I'm face down on the cool desert floor, the sheriff places the barrel of the shotgun to the back of my head.

"Scorpions, coyotes and buzzards three-way in your brains if you so much as flinch," he says.

Steel toe boots tickle my ribs before he lifts me to my feet and guides me to the cage in the back of the Jeep.

"Why'd you kill him?" Sheriff asks with a smile. "He diddle your wife? Owe you too much money? Piss on granny?"

Riding in the back of the Jeep with a lump on my head, busted ribs, and a new lease on life, the raging sun appears on the horizon through the impossible darkness.

"Water?" I ask.

"You give me that sweet and tender little confession, and I buy you a bucket of KFC and some mashed potatoes. Probably your best scenario. Otherwise, I beat the living confession out of you. Which would you prefer? Chicken or an ass-kickin'?"

"How about a lawyer?"

"What'd you say? Sorry, I got this bad hearing in my ear. I didn't hear that," he says. "Found you with a shovel in your hand, and a dead man in a hole. You either come clean, or I feed you to my hungry boots and splatter your dumb-shit brains all over the cacti. Choice is yours."

Similar to my confession, my time in County is brief. Clothed in orange prison garb with my hands and feet bound, I enter court. The judge looks down at me, clicking his teeth. I don't say a word. A circus clown in a sharkskin suit speaks the language of horseshit for me.

"Five years in Hawthorn," the judge says and lets the hammer drop. "Next case."

Cuffed between two barrel-chested sheriffs, I wait in the pissing rain.

"'Bout goddamn time," One of the sheriff's says, pushing the back of my neck towards a bus's opening door as the airbrakes hiss.

"Who we got?" A sheriff asks, sitting in the front of the bus with a clipboard.

"Soaked son of a bitch named Jaxon Ryker," the other sheriff says.

"Climb aboard, son," the sheriff with the clipboard says.

The sheriff pushes me through the metal door. Down the aisle, there are no open seats as the bus grinds out the parking lot. Prisoners sit two to a bench on both sides. I trip on a foot, but catch myself before eating floor. Sitting alone in the back, a large inmate with a baldhead and a scar running from his forehead to his chin hogs a bench.

"Push over," I say.

Scar Head ignores me, kicking a leg onto my seat. I knock his foot away and sit. He grabs my shirt, and a bolt of red lightening arcs across my mind as I head-butt Scar Head so hard his nose explodes. He keeps to his side of the bench for the remainder of the ride.

The bus descends into a canyon, grinding gears ache around hairpin turns as we slide down the devil's gullet. On the desert floor, we arrive at a tall fence topped with barbwire, and a series of checkpoints. The bus parks in a lot, and we exit single file into the rain. Looming watchtowers with spotlights circle the perimeter.

The sheriffs herd us into a gray colored box-shaped building. Inside reminds me of a high school gym without basketball hoops. The guards line us against the wall.

"Welcome to Hawthorn Adult Correctional Facility," A man says, stepping from the shadows, and dressed in a three-piece suit. "I'm Warden Hayes. There are no gangs here, and there are no individuals in Hawthorn. You had a name on the outside, but you fucked that up. Now you're not even a number. Now you are a smudge of dried shit the butt wipe missed."

After the warden's uplifting speech, the guards walk me to a small concrete cell with a bunk bed. I crash on the bottom mattress, thinking of Sarah. I need to get ahold of Tommy, and tell him to give her my earnings from my last win.

"Hooch?" A gravelly voice asks, a hand dangling a plastic water bottle filled with brown liquid from the bunk above.

"Looks like mud."

"They call me Rotgut. I make prison wine," A squat little man says, hopping to the ground.

"Tastes like dog shit," I say after a sip.

"But it fucks you up, so it's in demand. I trade for smokes, which I sell for cash that I use to bribe the guards, so I don't have to fight."

"Fight?"

"Hawthorn ain't public. This house of detention is a private for-profit institution."

"So what?"

"You ain't here to do time. You're here to fight. You a fighter?"

"Yeah."

"I can't fight, so I brew toilet hooch. You want me to show you how I make it?"

"No. The guards put on illegal fights?"

"It's bigger than the guards, though they'll probably take the fall if the public ever finds out about this place. Warden runs the pit. Makes a fuck-ton off high rolling European gamblers. If you ain't making toilet wine to stay out the pit, you best be hitting the weights because they gonna pull your card."

Rotgut is spot on. A week into pumping iron, a guard writes a tournament bracket on a filthy chalkboard in the yard. Inmates elbow in to see who's listed, and it doesn't take long for word to circulate that Charlie Knuckles' name is present.

"What happens if I refuse?" I ask Rotgut that night, lying in our respective bunks.

"They put you in the pit anyway. Guy on the other side of the cage is more than willing to tear your ass off, and make you wear it as a hat. It ain't all shitty, though. You landed in a tourney."

"So?"

"Winner gets a fight contract in a premier fight league."

"You mean…"

"Yep, freedom. Before you get your hopes up, you need to know something: Corbin Kane's on the other side of that bracket."

"Who?"

"Crazy motherfucker never loses. Big as a bull elephant and strong as a gorilla. Went ape-shit batty on angel dust, and killed his entire family. Wife, kids, even his ma and pa. He was undefeated as a pro. Ten plus knockouts."

For the first fight, I draw a big guy goes by Crusher. Several guards lead me into the gymnasium. The floor is packed with inmates, and in the middle of the room, lights illuminate a fighting cage. Men in suits sit in the bleachers, intently watching the show. I'm checked for weapons and then placed inside the cage.

Crusher enters the cage as inmates chant, 'to the death … to the death … to the death.' There is no referee. We take the center of the ring. The crispness of Crusher's jab surprises me. The speed and accuracy by which he pops it into my face tips me to his pugilistic abilities. I have to hurry and close the distance before he finds his range and timing. If he gets my range before I get the clinch, he'll start landing combinations, and bust me up.

I lunge, but underestimate his footwork. He dodges, making me pay for my telegraphed attempt by firing hooks into my mid-section. My ribs haven't recovered from the sheriff's steal toe boots in the desert. I wince and take a knee as my bones crack. A roar goes up on the floor at the sight of my weakness. Crusher dances around with his hands down, grinning and winking at me. I may be down but I sure as hell ain't out. An image of Sarah pops into my head. She's wearing only panties. My resolve hardens, and I climb to my feet through the pain.

Before Crusher gets his hands up, I rocket a high kick into the side of his head. I follow all the way through, and by the time my foot comes back down on the mat, Crusher's face is splattered across the floor. I can jump on him, and go for the kill, but instead, I try to open the cage door. There is no way Crusher recovers from that perfectly timed kick, and the ensuing head trauma.

The door remains locked. Crusher tries to gain his footing, but his equilibrium is off kilter. He stumbles across the cage, biffing his face into the metal links, and collapsing to his knees. In desperation, he lunges at me, but I step to the side. He misses by a good two feet.

I walk over to him, and put my foot on his back. The crowd goes ballistic, chanting, "Kill! Kill! Kill!" I bend down, put my arm around his neck, and choke him into unconsciousness, but I release my death grip on his throat as he blacks out. He crumples on the mat like a napkin after a hotdog. I sit against the fence in the opposite corner until the guards unlock the gate. I try to walk out, but I'm met with cudgels, and I join my bested competitor in unconsciousness.

When I come to, I'm soaking wet on a damp concrete floor. My face and ribs are swollen and sore. My tongue feels three sizes too big, and my thirst is intolerable. The door unlocks, and two guards lift me to my feet, and drag me into a room. On the table sits a sweaty pitcher of ice water. Instincts have me moving toward the hydrating liquid, but a guard's nightstick has different ideas.

While mourning my newly inflicted injuries, I notice the others in the room.

"Be a shame to damage you outside the cage," Warden Hayes says in a gold suit. "Give Charlie Knuckles here the works."

Several men, wearing black suits and sunglasses, sit quietly in the corner. I expect more of the ass whooping treatment as two massive guards yank me to my feet, but instead, it's the opposite. I'm given a glass of water, medical treatment for my wounds, and painkillers for the pain. A guard hands me a bag of McDonald's as I enter my new cell that seems more like a fancy hotel room.

A PlayStation is plugged into a flat screen television, hanging on the wall. The bed has clean sheets and a blanket, and the toilet has its own little room. A small refrigerator is filled with shit beer. I crack a Bud, wash down some hydrocodone, and smash the McDonald's: A six-pack of McNuggets with honey dipping sauce, a Big Mac, fries and an apple pie. Collapsing onto bed with a bowling ball in my stomach, I sink into the land of hushaby.

When I wake, a man stands over me. I focus on the steaming cup of coffee in his hand. He holds it out. Eagerly, I take the coffee and drink it as fast as its temperature allows. When the hot coffee is in my belly, I lean back against the wall.

"Hell of a fight," the warden says in a silver suit. "You're not the typical, one fighting style, meathead fighter in this joint. You flow effortlessly from one discipline to the next based on the nuances of the situation."

"I play a lot of golf on the outside," I say, feeling the coffee move to my bowels.

"Do you enjoy the luxury wing?"

"Sure."

"Then keep winning."

Among the amenities I now enjoy, I receive access to a private gym. Corbin also trains there. Corbin has the plushest cell in the detention facility, replete with kitchen and shower.

"You can't beat me," Corbin says with a smirk as he curled a massive dumbbell. "I been watching you, and I just don't see it. I got you by fifty pounds. You got no wrestling and your standup's a joke. They should call you Charlie Pillows. Don't take it personally, but I'm gonna clown your ass in front of the warden, and bitch slap you back to the commons in one of those halo head braces."

"I don't take it personally," I say. "So, you shouldn't either when I outwrestle you before knocking your dumb ass out."

"Good luck with that," Corbin says, and flexes in front of the mirror, his massive tanned muscles rippling on his arms and chest.

My next fight I'm in the cage with a karate expert named John "The Iguana" Cykes. His footwork is good, cutting diagonal angles, and his strikes crack like lightening. A head kick sits me on the floor. The next shot puts me out, but the shot after that wake me up. Something about my head bouncing on the canvas like a basketball with each punch causes me to come to my senses.

The Iguana tries to keep me down, but my sheer willpower is too much for him, and we return to our feet. He tries to create distance, and to tag me with outside shots. I counter by recklessly storming in to close the distance. He tags me with another lightning bolt, and I splatter face first, but again, my off switch turns back on when my head jars the ground. I eat knees and kicks as I climb to my feet.

This time, I cut off the cage, and pin him against the fence. We grapple, and I land a series of dirty boxing blows to the head and body. The Iguana slips from my grasp, and throws a hard spinning elbow, catching me flush on the jaw. I lose feeling in my legs, and slump against the fence. The Iguana lands repeatedly on my face. I detach from my body. Looking down, I see myself losing the fight, and possibly my life. In the front row, I see men in black suits, and the judge that sentenced me to Hawthorn. The incarcerated crowd cheers at my impending demise like demons in hell.

As my head ping-pongs on the canvas, my numb arms flail like a marionette. Suddenly, I'm back in my body. Sarah is taking a hot shower. The pain shocks me to my feet. The Iguana throws a scissor kick. He misses by a mile, and falls hard on his ass. As he stands, I slide my arm under his neck. My hands clasped, and I squeeze and squeeze until time vanishes, and there is only the brutal crack of the guard's club, separating me from my prey.

I wake up the next day in the infirmary. A tube is up my urethra, and another is in my wrist. A day later, I'm back in my cell, eating KFC. A concussive fog settles around me. Corbin won his fight handily, and we are slated to fight for the contract. I front like everything's cool, but Corbin and Warden Hayes know I'm wounded. Sometimes though, moments of clarity occur during the threat of death, and amazing shit happens. I have a tall order in front of me, but I'm not counting myself out. A cornered animal is the most dangerous animal.

My suite is upgraded to cellular as a result of my last win. A burner waits for me on the bed. I flip open the phone, and call Tommy.

"Hey, who's this?"

"Hey, Tommy, listen it's Jaxon. I need a favor."

"Jesus, Charlie, what time is it?" Tommy asks. "Jax is on the phone. You want to talk to him?"

"Where the hell you been?" Sarah demands on the other end.

"You in bed with Tommy?" I ask.

"That's right," she says. "You up and disappeared on my ass, so now I'm fucking him."

"Hey, Jax," Tommy says. "Sorry about all that. I hope we're cool. Hey, man. How's Hawthorn?"

I hang up the phone with the heel of my boot, squashing the electronic device like a bug. It hurts to know that Tommy is with my girl, but in another way, it hardens me, helps me clear my mind. There is nothing waiting for me in my former life. There is also nothing but pain, suffering and death waiting for me in prison. My only hope of escaping my dismal fate is to win the tournament, sign the contract, and walk out of this nightmare a free man.

The next few days I take it easy. I sit in my cell, wearing sunglasses, pretending to play *Grand Theft Auto*, but really, I'm sweating and zoning out. My brain isn't right, and I know it will not be healed come fight night. Corbin is a huge motherfucker, full of muscle and shit talk. How am I to beat this family-murdering ogre?

Wearing an opal suit, Warden Hayes and several men in black enter my cell.

"Congratulations on making it to the finals, young man," the warden says, and the other men stare silently, taking notes. "Many had their doubts about you in the beginning. Not being able to take Crusher's life, but that perception changed after your fight with the Iguana."

Didn't realize I'd killed the poor bastard. The last thing I remember is squeezing his neck before waking up in the hospital.

They let me eat whatever I want the night before the big fight, kind of a last meal sort of deal. I take down a big New York sirloin steak, potatoes, and a can of beer. I murder the beer in one long chug, and let out a satisfying belch. Sometimes life has a funny way of putting you in the right place at the right time. I'm about to win my second straight turkey, and win a fight contract. All I have to do is beat a multi-organization champion who murdered his family.

They lead me into the cage. In the front row, I see the sheriff from out in the desert, sitting next to the judge that sentenced me. The glaring spotlights mix with the harsh fluorescents overhead, triggering a migraine headache. I ask for some water, but my request is met with jeers. The crowd goes nuts as Corbin enters the cage. His impeccable muscles shine with grease.

The bell rings. Showing no respect, Corbin flies across the cage. I wing him with a perfectly timed hook that sets him slightly off balance. Confusion registers on his face. It's not supposed to go this way, but I'm letting him know that I don't give a fuck.

I follow up the hook with a jab, jab, head kick, and Corbin's legs wobble, but before I can commit further damage, his eyes clear, and he regains his composure. He digs for a takedown, and puts me on my back. I try forcing my way up to my feet, but Corbin is heavy on top. I turtle up as he rains down hammer fists. I eat a few big ones. When the stars start twinkling in my vision, I grab the next punch to my face, and wrap my arms around his extended arm, locking in a Kimura.

Again, Corbin looks confused as I use the submission attempt to reverse position. Easily, he pushes me away, and we end up back on our feet. Corbin bombards me with heavy leather. I roll with or block most of the shots, but a few find their mark, and my legs almost buckle. Moving away, I try to breathe and clear my head, but Corbin is relentless. Smelling blood, he moves in for the kill.

The pain in my head explodes with each shot. Blood splatters on the canvas. Wobbling back, I stumble into the fence. If there'd been a referee, he'd have stopped the fight here, because I'm out on my feet. Like a zombie, the repetitions I drilled with Tommy so many times take over: Grapple for an underhook, but give up the other underhook … Grapple for an underhook, but give up the other underhook … Grapple for an underhook, but give up the other underhook …

Corbin steps back, breathing heavy. I'm a bloody heap, but still alive. Corbin is gassing. He spent his tank on the flurry, thinking he had me for sure, but I'm a tough motherfucker, as tough as they come. I move forward, easily avoiding his tired and slow punches. I initiate the clench. He takes a deep breath. I take the right underhook, but give him the left underhook. Corbin is an old school wrestler, so me forfeiting the left underhook is strange to him. He is used to heavy grappling for that position, so again, amid the sweat and panting, confusion registers on Corbin's face.

He has the underhook, but my left hand is free. I use my free hand to grab the back of his head. When I do this, he tries to push away, and I blast a hard upper cut with my right hand. It connects clean with Corbin's chin, putting my opponent flat on his ass. The confusion on his face morphs into shock, followed by fear and desperation. Now it is my turn to dribble a head on the floor with punches.

Corbin's body goes limp, and he loses consciousness, but I keep punching him. I keep punching him for his wife and kids and his mom and dad. I keep punching him for what Fran did to me, for what Tommy and Sarah did to me. I keep punching him for the contract and for my freedom. I keep punching his face until it is gone, and the bones in my hands break, until there is nothing left of Corbin's face, but a bloody flesh soup. Eventually, the guards enter the cage, and knock me to the ground with their nightsticks, cuff me, and carry me to the infirmary where the doctor gives me a shot of something that puts me to sleep.

When I wake up, I am in my prison suite. Warden Hayes, wearing a Burberry suit, and the men in black stand around my bed.

"One hell of a fight, Knuckles. You've exceeded expectations. These men want to sign you to a premier fighting league. What do you think about that?"

"And my freedom?"

"You've earned a full pardon. I just need you to sign these papers. Hell, these men will even arrange a limousine to pick you up."

It isn't easy signing the contract with two broken hands, but I manage it. I don't want to show weakness, but the sobs erupt out of a deep and dark place way down inside my core. This is everything I've worked so hard for. No more sleeping on the mats at the gym. No more showering in the janitor's closet. No more shoplifting food. I've eaten and slept better in prison than before incarceration. Now I'm leaving prison a fucking rock star, a back-to-back turkey wining motherfucker with his own fighting contract for a premiere fight league.

"Hello," one of the men in black suits says, stepping forward. "I'm Aslen. How you say, impressive, no?"

"Thanks," I say embarrassed, wiping away the tears.

"Yes, yes," Aslen says in an Eastern European accent. "You eh, have the big balls, eh."

"Put me in a cage with anybody in the world, and I'll walk out the winner," I say.

The next morning, I'm taken from my cell, and given a tailored suit and tie, dress-shoes, and designer sunglasses. I've never owned such nice garments. The best I did for myself on the outside was a gym t-shirt, some board shorts, rotten flip-flops, and a raggedy ass pair of jeans when it was cold. Now I'm Don Fucking Smooth.

A guard on either side walks me through the front door. In the yard, the miserable pressure from the desert's blistering heat pushes down on me. The airbrakes of a bus wheeze, and the door swings open. Orange clad prisoners with angry faces disembark from the transportation vehicle: Men that look like they want to kick ass, men looking for a way to beat the shit out of the thing standing between them and freedom. Poor bastards don't stand a chance.

I duck into a black limo. A little wooden box sits on the seat with my name on a little tag. I open the gift, and find a nickel-plated pistol.

"Thanks, guys," I say, admiring the weapon. "Where we heading?"

"Private jet."

"Vegas?"

The men shrug, and light cigarettes. One of them hands me a beer.

"We are embarrassed to tell you this Mr. Knuckles. We thought you knew."

The limo blasts down a fire road as billowing clouds of dirt rise from the back tires. A small airstrip appeared on the horizon. We park next to a private jet.

"The organization you now fight for is in Gronzy."

"Where the fuck is Gronzy?" I ask and climb out of the limo into the howling wind. "Jersey?"

We climb the stairs. I stop at the door to the fuselage, look out at the heat waves radiating off the desert floor, chug my beer, and board the private jet.

Don't Be Next

Abel gunned his Harley around the sharp curves as he ascended through the Santa Cruz Mountains. At the summit, he spied a green cross next to an eatery with a sign that read 'Coffee, Soda, Pizza, Beer,' so he turned left against oncoming traffic, and rumbled into the parking lot. After a hotdog and two beers, Abel sauntered next door to the pot dispensary, and used his medical marijuana card to buy several pre-rolled joints. Outside, two motorcycles were parked near his hog. He felt the knife on his hip as he scanned the area. Two clean-cut old guys carried their helmets into the restaurant. Abel removed his hand from the blade, and started his Harley. The exhaust pipes roared, turning heads in the parking lot. Popping a toothpick into the side of his mouth, Abel burped and thundered down the mountain.

He was early for his rendezvous at the Crow's Nest, so he cruised to the lighthouse on the Westside, parking near the bathrooms at the edge of a field. Abel crossed the street, and joined a crowd of spectators at the railing above the sea cliffs. A small pack of surfers bobbed just outside the break, taking turns paddling into massive waves. Only a handful of skilled watermen dared challenge these rolling seas—with one exception. Dangerously near the crags, a man in a red wetsuit on a long blue foam board attempted to make it past the breakers. He struggled against the strong current as continuous walls of whitewater dragged him towards the rocks.

Spectators and lifeguards along the cliff yelled at the floundering man, instructing him to get out of the water, but he continued his losing endeavor against the massive swells. During a lull, he paddled beyond the rocky point into a hazardous stretch of surf. A lifeguard on a Jet Ski approached, but enormous waves kept him from rescuing the man in the red wetsuit.

Caught in the impact zone, the man in the red wetsuit was plunged under the torrent. Upon resurfacing, his foam board was in pieces, and he had been dragged into an inlet that was surrounded by large jagged rocks.

A sign posted above on the cliff next to the railing read:

Don't Be Next
Since 1965, 103 people have drowned
along our coastal cliffs and beaches.
Many of these deaths were preventable.
STAY BEHIND FENCES
STAY AWAY FROM CLIFF EDGES

The onlookers watched the battering of the man in the red wetsuit against the ragged seawall. A silence fell over the crowd at the sight of another human's impending demise. During a momentary break in the surf, a lifeguard rescue swimmer reached the man in the red wetsuit, and paddled him to a floatation device hanging from the back of the nearby Jet Ski as a giant foam beast moved in for the kill. The crowd cheered as the small watercraft barely cleared the monstrous water wall. A moment later, a thunderous clap of angry white rapids erupted into the cove amid plumes of hissing mist.

The spectators' opinions turned from concern to disapproval. Words like "kook" and "idiot" were used to describe the inexperienced surfer. Putting his hand in his pocket, Abel felt the joints he bought on the summit. He still had time to kill, so he crossed the street, and entered the field.

He wandered along a path to a row of cypress trees while contemplating the near drowning. Despite witnessing the miraculous rescue, Abel was disappointed the man had cheated his watery grave. It would have made a great story to tell the Fighting Bastards.

The incident brought back a memory from Abel's childhood. His mother took him to the beach in Santa Cruz for the day when he was ten. She rented a surfboard, he paddled into the water in front of the boardwalk, and climbed to his feet on the first wave. He remembered how proud his mother was, and he knew someday he'd be a surfer. Several months later, his mother died in a car accident in San Jose, and many years passed before Abel returned to the beach.

He found a knotty cypress tree growing low and sideways that functioned as a bench. Empty beer cans and fast-food wrappers littered the ground. He lit a joint, thinking about the importance of tonight. Gaining hangout status with the North Valley Fighting Bastards had taken Abel longer than expected, but persistency, and a penchant for scoring coke had gotten him noticed by the gang's leaders.

For months, Abel had been the grunt, cleaning bikes, and spending his own money on beer runs. Now, he was a prospect, and Loco Dave was his sponsor. Hopefully, after tonight, he'd earn his patch and become a full-fledged member. When the joint ended, he returned to his bike, and headed for the Crow's Nest.

At a red light, Abel saw people drinking beer on an outdoor patio near the railroad tracks. The smell of hamburger meat permeated the air, arousing Abel's appetite. The light turned green, and he crossed the harbor bridge, and found an open spot in the Crow's Nest parking lot. Although it was early, the restaurant was crowded. Senior citizens clogged the lobby, waiting for tables.

"Can I help you?" a beautiful young hostess asked Abel.

"Nah," he replied, and ascended a set of stairs.

Loco Dave and several other members of the Fighting Bastards leaned against the bar on the second floor. Abel sat on a stool by Loco Dave and ordered a Bud.

"Make that a round," Loco Dave said without acknowledging Abel.

The bartender glanced at Abel. Abel nodded in the affirmative, and gazed out the windows at the harbor. A large sailboat was returning from a day on the turgid sea just before sunset. Abel's stomach grumbled. He wanted a cheeseburger, but thought better of it. Ordering food meant ordering the gang food.

After finishing his beer, Abel went downstairs to use the bathroom. On the floor by the urinal, he noticed a little baggy containing blue pills. He didn't know what they were, but he pocketed the find before unzipping to take a leak.

As he reentered the bar, the sun's sinking rays colored the skyline gold, pink and purple above the tumultuous expanse. Everybody quietly observed the pleasing sunset except the Fighting Bastards. Dirty Dog thought a guy wearing an O'Neal hat was staring.

"You got a problem, bitch?" Dirty Dog asked.

"Huh?" the man in the O'Neal hat said.

Dirty Dog stood up, knocking over his stool. The man in the O'Neil hat puffed out his chest, stepping forward, but before the situation escalated any further, the Crow's Nest's bouncers intervened, forcibly ushering the Fighting Bastards down the stairs, and out the front door.

Dirty Dog was livid. He wanted to stab every last one of those motherfuckers inside. Abel felt it was a good time to show the boys the pills. He figured it might break the tension.

"Look what I found on the floor in the pisser," Abel said to Loco Dave, handing him the little baggy.

"You know what these are?" Loco Dave asked, examining the pharmaceuticals.

"No."

"Hell. You're in luck," Loco Dave said. "You just found some speedballs."

Abel figured he'd have to share the uppers, so he was surprised when Loco Dave handed him back the baggy.

"Anybody else?" Abel asked.

"No, man. Your find. Go ahead and pop a few. You'll be climbing the walls in no time."

Abel swallowed a few of the pills without the aid of beer. He took it as a sign he was moving into the ranks of the Fighting Bastards, but as soon as the pills went down, Loco Dave chuckled.

"Numb nuts here thinks he took speed," Loco Dave said.

"What was it?"

"Boner meds," Loco Dave said, and everybody, even Dirty Dog, laughed. "You just took a shit load of Viagra."

"If your dick don't go down in four hours, you gotta seek medical attention," Dirty Dog said.

"Hey, Road Kill, what's the boat's name again?" Loco Dave asked.

"The Lucky Lady," Road Kill said.

"I'll say."

As they walked along the harbor, doubts about burning the Grim Reapers brewed in Abel's mind. The Grim Reapers were the Fighting Bastards rivals. The Grim Reapers held a monopoly on the heroin trade in North Valley, which was a huge thorn in the Fighting Bastards' side. The Fighting Bastards couldn't find a San Jose supplier, nor could they figure out where the Grim Reapers scored their smack—that is until they met Eddie Sanchez.

Eddie Sanchez was a low-level soldier for the Grim Reapers, but when he discovered his wife was boning down with his biker buddies, Eddie went straight to the Hole. The Hole was a North Valley dive bar, and the Fighting Bastards' hangout. Road Kill recognized Eddie, and was about to whip his ass when Eddie convinced him otherwise. He bought Road Kill a beer and explained how the Grim Reapers' connection worked. The heroin came in through the Santa Cruz harbor on a sailboat named the Lucky Lady. Eddie told Road Kill when the next shipment arrived. He also mentioned that the Grim Reapers didn't pick up the shit until the next day, so if the Fighting Bastards wanted, they could retrieve the heroin first.

Abel jumped at the chance to participate in the raid as soon as Loco Dave told him about the plan. This was Abel's chance to prove his loyalty and worth, and to finally earn his patch, and become a member of the Fighting Bastards.

They stopped at a small fenced off pier with a locked gate.

"Dirty Dog," Loco Dave said. "Work your magic."

Dirty Dog took a chisel and a hammer out of his bag. After three powerful knocks on the lock, the gate swung open. The Fighting Bastards drew their pistols along the dock and approached the Lucky Lady.

"What the fuck?" A man in a gray hoodie with a goatee said, sticking his head out of the large sailboat's hatch.

Loco Dave pistol-whipped Gray Hoodie, and knocked him back into the boat's cabin. The Fighting Bastards piled in, holding Gray Hoodie and another man sitting at a small table hostage.

"Where's the shit?" Loco Dave asked.

Neither man responded, so Loco Dave took out his knife, and sliced off a piece of Gray Hoodie's left ear.

"Come on Evander Holyfield, where's the fucking horse?" Loco Dave asked. "I'll murder you and your butt buddy here, if you don't hand it over. Think I'm joking? Abel, slit this motherfucker's throat."

Abel removed his knife, and loomed over Gray Hoodie, staring into the man's piercing blue eyes before placing the knife to his throat and cutting a deep bloody line across the neck. Gray Hoodie remained silent, except for a gurgling noise as his eyes rolled into the back of his head.

"You're next," Loco Dave said to the other man.

"Wait," he pleaded. "Give me a second."

With trembling hands, the man unscrewed a hidden cubby in the wall, removed two large bags, and handed them to Loco Dave. Loco Dave cut one of them open, and snorted a dab of the whitish powder.

"Jackpot," he said. "Abel, kill this motherfucker too."

This time Abel didn't make the mistake of looking into his victim's eyes. He went straight for the throat with his blade. When the job was finished, Abel was alone. His compatriots' boots thudded outside on the wooden dock. Abel wiped his blade clean on a curtain, and fled the Lucky Lady, wishing he'd parked his bike closer as the rumbling of the Fighting Bastards' fleeing motorcycles faded into the distance.

The Crow's Nest's parking lot was well lit and full of automobiles. Abel slipped between two rows of cars, and noticed a crowd gathered around his bike. He pushed through the throng, and found his Harley under the rear bumper of a large white luxury sedan. A trembling old man with snow-white hair hunched over the automobile's steering wheel. Abel cursed, punching the automobile several times, leaving smears of blood on the side of the car. The crowd stepped back as the biker dragged his Harley out from under the sedan.

He leaned his hog upright, but the handlebars were askew. He tried the kick-start several times, but the engine would not catch. Abel threw his bike down amid a torrent of expletives. The old man exited his vehicle, and approached, but Abel shoved him to the ground, and fled onto a nearby beach scattered with bonfires.

Abel crossed the street, ducking into a residential area. He wandered through the neighborhood with an erection in his pants. At the railroad tracks, he made his way back over the harbor bridge. Looking behind, he saw a dark figure in the distance. Abel quickened his pace until he came to an underpass just before a trestle. He peered over his shoulder again, but didn't see anybody.

As he crossed the trestle, the bright lights of the Boardwalk emphasized the bloodstains on his clothes. Tourists parted like the Red Sea as Abel passed the casino. Just before the wharf, he ducked into a public bathroom, and looked in the mirror. Blood speckled his beard and leather jacket. He washed his face and hands in the sink as a homeless man entered.

"Spare a dollar?"

"Twenty bucks for your shirt," Abel said.

Abel discarded his leather jacket—something he never would have imagined an hour ago—and put on the homeless man's putrid garment. It was grimy and damp, tattered and stained yellow with perspiration. The smell made Abel gag.

"Where do I catch the bus to San Jose?" He asked.

"Take a right at the roundabout," the homeless man said, eyeing the blood-stained leather jacket.

As Abel exited the bathroom, he had the sensation of being followed, but it was impossible to know for sure in such a crowded area. He crossed the roundabout, making his way to the metro station. The bus to San Jose was just about to leave as he arrived. He paid the seven-dollar fare, and took the last available seat in the front. An old woman stood up and walked to the back after he sat down beside her.

The bus pulled out of the station, and Abel closed his eyes. He opened them again when his thoughts returned to the Lucky Lady. Abel trembled at the blue eyes and the gurgling sound. He cussed, and the passengers around him shifted uneasily in their seats. The bus driver turned his head back for a moment, and asked if everything was okay? Abel looked out the window. At the summit, he saw the eatery he had stopped at on his way into town. It was dark and closed.

He thought about his wife. How foolish he was to make her play second fiddle to an outlaw motorcycle gang. He couldn't wait for her to pick him up at the station. He would start treating her better. He would start tonight by working off this Viagra. She always liked hitting the sack, but for some reason, he rarely gave it to her anymore. He was always too busy trying to bang the biker babes at the Hole.

His mind shifted back to the blue eyes and the gurgling sound.

"If you don't quiet down," the bus driver said. "And stop disturbing the other passengers, I'll kick you off this bus in the middle of nowhere."

Abel's mind switched to his job. He was a plumber. He had hated his work for the past several years, but now it didn't seem so bad. It paid well, and kept him busy. He had dreamed of quitting when he joined the Fighting Bastards, but now that he had tasted the life, working on those shit pipes didn't seem so terrible anymore.

As the bus pulled into San Jose, Abel stood up. The cool night air splashed across his face as the bus door opened. He entered the station in search of a payphone. At the far end of the depot, he called his wife from a booth.

"Hello?" She answered.

"Hey, babe."

"Where you been?"

"I'll tell you all about it when you get me. I'm stranded at the San Jose train station."

"Be right there."

"Thanks, babe. Love you," he said, and hung up the phone.

He would make it up to her. All those times he wasn't there, or had been shitty to her—he would make amends for his behavior. The feeling of atonement afforded him a moment's relief from the evening's chaos, but then a thought crept into his head that turned him pale with fear. Soon, the police would discover the bodies on the Lucky Lady. He'd left his Harley near the crime scene, and it was smeared with the victims' blood. It wouldn't be long before they rubbed two brain cells together and came looking for him.

He walked outside, and sat on a bench near the curb. Abel stood up each time a set of headlights went by in anticipation of his wife's car. It would take her a while to drive from North Valley, but Abel wasn't thinking clearly.

He stood as a set of headlights approached. A vehicle stopped at the curb, but it was a van, so he sat down cussing to himself. The side door slid open, and several men in hoodies piled out, grabbed Abel and forced him into the vehicle. The door slid shut. Something metallic cracked against his head, and he went unconscious.

When he woke, it was dark. He lay on his back on the floorboard as the van rounded a series of sharp curves. Every inch of his body hurt, yet Abel still had an erection.

Eventually the van came to a stop, and the driver cut the motor. The hooded men sat in silence for several minutes, smoking cigarettes, and looking into the darkness.

"Coast is clear," Loco Dave said.

The van's side door slid open, and the Fighting Bastards dragged Able from the automobile, towards the railing as a thunderous clap reverberated through the salty air amid plumes of hissing mist.

Boundaries

For about a year, Alec had complained about a large leaning pine on my property that threatened a structure near the back of his lot. He kept pressing me to hire an arborist to remove the tilting tower, but I didn't think the problem urgent. He even gave me the phone number for his brother's tree removal service. His kin's quote seemed steep, so I declined.

In the night, a nasty storm soaked the soil, and the reclining pine toppled, destroying the fence and Alec's greenhouse. In the morning, I rang my neighbor's bell.

"Yeah?" Alec asked, through the screen.

"Tree out back came down last night—"

"How many times I tell you to fell that son of a bitch," he said, slamming the door in my face.

I snapped pictures of the wreckage with my digital camera for insurance purposes. Alec cussed loudly on the other side of the destruction, documenting his mangled greenhouse with an old Polaroid camera.

The next morning, the buzz of chainsaws woke me. Alec's brother Charlie and some rough characters were sectioning the fallen tree and removing the wood from the property line. In my haste, I knotted my bathrobe, slipped on my wife's pink bunny slippers, and flung open the sliding glass door to the backyard. I tried getting Charlie's attention, but he kept sawing until I stood over him, dangerously close to the spinning chain.

"Careful," Charlie said, cutting the gas, and spitting chaw onto one of my wife's pink bunny slippers. "I slip, and this blade goes right through you."

"What the hell is this?" I demanded.

"Tree removal," Charlie said.

"I didn't authorize it."

Alec approached with his hellhound.

"Let these boys alone, Hugh." Alec said.

"I didn't okay this."

"No shit," Alec said, and his dog growled at me. "Had you dealt with this problem in a timely fashion, we wouldn't be in this mess. You knew this tree was a danger to my property, and you did squat, so now you'll foot the bill."

"The hell I will," I said. "You'll be hearing from my lawyer."

"Calm down, Rebel," Alec said to his massive Rottweiler. "I don't like Hugh neither, but I can't let you at him. He still needs to pay for the tree removal, the fence, and my damaged property."

"I got a buddy can do these fence repairs cheap," Charlie said.

"I'm not saying another word until I talk to my lawyer, so stop what you're doing and get off my property before I call the cops," I demanded.

Alec smiled, and Charlie fired up his chainsaw. I stomped back to my house, slipped off my wife's brown bunny slippers, and entered through the sliding glass door.

Moscow, my five-year-old son, heard me swearing, and repeated the profanity. Lori told me to calm down, be rational, and discuss the situation with Alec like a civilized being. I stomped into my office and emailed the photos of the downed tree and the busted fence to my insurance company before calling my lawyer.

"Dave, Hugh here. How's it going?" I asked over the phone.

"I'm drowning in alimony and child support from two different marriages, and I'm on trial for a forgery case, and I don't mean I'm trying the case," Dave said. "I mean I'm personally being sued for forging several deeds. The prosecution has a forensics expert taking the stand against me."

"Hey, listen," I said. "A tree on my property fell into my neighbor's yard. Am I liable?"

"I wouldn't worry. Your neighbor's insurance will probably cover the damages. Why did it fall?"

"It started leaning that way a year or so ago."

"Did you know the tree was unstable?"

"Um—well, uh, yeah."

"Can your neighbor prove you knew the tree was unstable?"

"Yeah. Alec kept complaining about it. His arborist brother quoted me something like three grand to take it down, so I told him to take a hike."

"Sounds like you're at fault, and he'll probably sue you for liability. Also, from what I understand, three grand's a pretty good deal to take down a leaner."

"What should I do? He's already got his brother sawing and hauling away the tree."

"Contact your insurance company. Make them aware of the situation."

I bashed down the phone. Moscow stood beside me, holding a piece of paper.

"I druw it, daddy. It's you and the twee before it fall."

"Let's see," I said, snatching the coloring from his hands.

Although the art was crude, the poorly drawn tree leaned towards Alec's scribbly house. I crumpled the drawing into a wad, and threw it against the wall. Moscow screamed and ran to his mother. Lori confronted me, but I shut her down with a "now is not the time" glare just as Waffles rubbed against my leg. Snatching up the phone, I ignored the family cat, and dialed my insurance agent.

"Greg, Hugh here."

"Hey, Hugh. What can I help you with? Ah, shit."

"Everything okay?"

"Yeah. I just spilled hot coffee on my lap."

"Listen. A tree on my property fell into a neighbor's yard. I sent you some pictures."

"Give me a second … Let me bring up my email … Wow, that sucker's big," Greg said. "I'm guessing your neighbor's homeowner's insurance will cover the damage."

"You think Alec's insurance will cover the cost," I repeated, but my wife stared at me, shaking her head in the negative. "Hold on, my wife disagrees. Lori, what do you mean?"

"Carol told me Alec discontinued the family's homeowner's insurance several years back."

"Hey, Greg, Lori's telling me the neighbors don't have insurance."

"Christ," Greg said. "That puts us on the hook, but I have to tell you, we can only cover up to five hundred dollars. You'll have to pick up the rest."

"Five hundred dollars," I yelled into the phone. "What the hell have I been paying you crooks for all these years?"

"Calm down, Hugh. All the facts aren't in yet."

"The illusion of coverage?" I yelled into the phone, and smashed down the receiver.

My bad temper subsided over the next few days, and I tried not to think about the ordeal. I'd wait to see how Alec played his hand, and counter his move accordingly.

A week passed, and nothing happened. Alec's scuzzy brother removed the fallen tree, but the busted fence separating our properties remained an open wound.

One day, Alford wandered into our backyard. Alford was Alec and Carol's massive, hulking, barrel-chested, seventeen-year-old, mentally disabled son. Lori called Carol to inform her that Alford was in our backyard, and I went outside to talk to the boy.

"Hi, Alford," I said. "Are you supposed to be over here?"

"I like the kitty," he said, petting Waffles.

"Do your parents know where you are?" I asked.

"I pet the kitty."

"Do Alec and Carol know you're here?"

"I pet the kitty."

"Hey," Alec yelled from the broken fence line. "Get your ass over here, boy."

"But I pet the kitty."

"Goddamn it, Alford. Now."

"You should listen to your dad," I said. "Go home."

"Okay," Alford said. "Bye-bye, kitty."

He stood up, and I noticed tufts of cat hair stuck to Alford's fingers.

"Hey," I said to Alford, and grabbed Waffles. "What did you do?"

"I pet the kitty," he said, walking away.

"You killed the kitty," I said, holding Waffles' lifeless body.

"Get inside, boy," Alec said, grabbing Alford by the arm and leading him home.

Moscow was stricken with grief. He crawled under our bed and cried. Lori called Carol. They talked for a long time, and when Lori finally hung up the phone, I asked what Carol said.

"She said there was no way Alford killed Waffles, and she resented the accusation. She thinks the cat was already dead."

"Funny how Waffles made it a decade out here without so much as a scratch, but the fence goes down, the retard escapes, and our cat just miraculously happens to die?"

"Hugh, please don't use that word. Alford is severely autistic. Sometimes you can be so mean. You need to lighten up on Alec and his family, okay?"

"Carol's the one that needs to lighten up. She must weigh a ton."

"Knock it off, Hugh. I mean it. Carol said we owe Charlie three thousand for the tree."

"That redneck piece of shit's crazy if he thinks he's getting a dime out of me. We didn't hire him. The nerve of these people, they deny killing Waffles, and they charge us for work we don't want."

A few weeks slid by, and we hadn't heard from Alec. The fence was still down, but neither of us offered the other an olive branch, so the problem lingered like an infection.

One day as I returned home from work, Lori met me in the front yard. She said Alec's Rottweiler had mauled Moscow. I found my little boy on the couch, crying with a bloody towel wrapped around his head.

"Let's get you to the hospital," I said picking him up.

But then I set him down and called 911. Moscow needed immediate medical attention. An ambulance would provide help faster than us driving down the mountain, and the service would cost Alec substantially more in medical bills.

The emergency vehicle's sirens blared as it pulled into the driveway. Neighbors watched from their porches as my wounded little boy and his sobbing mother climbed into the ambulance. I stayed behind, so I could bring the car to the hospital.

In the kitchen, I gathered supplies. Tossing a box of Cheese-It crackers into a tote bag, I looked through the window. Alec slouched in my backyard, smoking a cigarette.

"Get off my property," I said, approaching.

"Rebel's a good boy," Alec said without moving.

"He's a regular saint," I said. "And Alford didn't kill Waffles either. You people are unbelievable."

"I'm hiring my brother's friend to fix the fence," Alec said, and took a drag from his cigarette.

"And you're paying for it too," I said. "Keep your monsters away from my family."

Alec looked at me, but didn't say anything. He smoked his cigarette down to the filter, crushed the butt under his boot, turned around, and walked into his yard. I snatched up the crumpled debris and hurled it, hitting Alec's back. He turned, cracking a sickly smile before disappearing into his house.

Moscow needed stiches in his scalp. We reported the incident to the police and animal control. When Moscow was released from the emergency room, we took him for ice cream.

The neighbors were on their porches as we parked in our driveway. Three police officers had Alec lying prone on his lawn. An empty whisky bottle and a shotgun lay nearby. They cuffed him and lifted him to his feet. He had murder in his eyes as the police led him to a patrol car.

I asked Hal, two houses down, what happened? He said animal control took Rebel. Alec was drunk in the street, waving a shotgun around, and screaming for revenge. Silence hung between us for a moment before Hal asked me about the broken fence in my backyard.

He said he'd fix it for a friendly price. Without another word, I turned and walked home.

One evening after work, I found several unknown men building a fence through the middle of my backyard.

"What the hell are you doing?" I yelled at the strange carpenters. "Get off my property, or I'm calling the police."

"Call 'em, so I can have you removed for trespassing," Alec said, smoking a cigarette. "I looked over the estate surveys, and noticed the boundaries were laid out wrong. You're standing on my property."

"The hell I am. If you don't stop building this fence immediately, I will sue the shit out of you."

"Go ahead. We'll see who's liable, dog killer."

"Your dog attacked my son."

"I'm surprised you didn't have Alford put down too."

"Unbelievable. Your son kills my cat, and your dog mauls my son and you try to make me feel bad."

"Rebel was a good boy."

"I can't speak for the neighborhood, but I've slept better without that mutt howling every morning at 4AM."

"I'll send you the bill for the fence and the greenhouse."

"And I'll wipe my ass with the bill, and use it as kindling to burn down this fence."

The sun sank below the mountain, so construction halted, but the argument continued into the darkness. Lori came out, tried to play peacemaker, and dragged me indoors, but not before I told Alec to take a flying fuck off a sinking turd.

The next morning, I called my lawyer.

"Dave, Hugh here."

"Hugh, can it wait?" Dave asked. "I'm due for a hearing in about ten minutes, and I need to go over some notes."

"My neighbor Alec claims the property line is wrong, and now he's building a fence through my backyard."

"Sounds like a boundary dispute. You need to compare deeds. If you can't come to an agreement, get a land survey."

"How much will that cost?"

"Hard to say. Find your deed, and call several estate firms. If you can prove your neighbor is encroaching, you can sue him. That's about all I can do for you right now."

I slammed down the phone just as the hammering out back began again. No way Alec would compare property deeds with me, and I didn't want to pay a survey team, so I figured I'd wait until the fence was built, and burn it down. Lori didn't think that was such a hot idea. Begrudgingly, I searched our filing cabinet for the deed, thinking I'd have to shell out for a survey after all, but then an idea kicked me square in the ass, and I slammed shut the cabinet.

The solution had been in front of my face the entire time and I just hadn't seen it, but now the answer to my woes showed like a beacon of hope upon a vengeful sea of neighborly wrath. When the tree fell, it took out the fence, but it also took out Alec's greenhouse. What the hell did Alec need a greenhouse for? We have some of the richest soil in the county. He wasn't growing tomatoes in there. He was growing something else. As a concerned citizen, I felt it my duty to report such activities to the proper authorities.

When the police officer arrived, I led him into my backyard, and I pointed to Alec's damaged greenhouse. From our vantage point, marijuana plants were visible.

The officer called the station, and a search warrant was issued within the hour.

The police found over fifty plants. Inside Alec's home, they discovered little plastic bags and scales, which showed intent to sell, bumping the crime up to a felony. They also discovered several unregistered firearms. Amid the spectating neighbors, Alec was handcuffed. Again, murder gleamed in his eyes as they stuffed him into a patrol car.

The next day, Lori drove Moscow into Scott's Valley to see a kid's movie. I grabbed a hammer and a crowbar, and tore down the fence while doing my best Ronald Reagan impersonation. "Mr. Gorbachev—tear down this wall." When I finished dismantling the palisade, I returned to the house, popped a beer, and plopped on the couch. Flipping on a golf tournament, I sat back in contentment.

Goddamn it felt good to beat that asshole. Life could finally get back to normal.

As I started to doze, the sliding glass door exploded. I snapped awake, thinking Alec posted bail, and would have his revenge via shotgun, but then I saw a large cobblestone on the living room floor amid the shards of broken glass.

In the backyard, I saw Carol lumbering back onto her property.

Hefting the stone with the intention of returning the favor, I noticed a faded and sienna Polaroid taped to the rock: My wife spread naked on a bed. Rebel curled at her feet.

Dead Meat

Dave and I worked the bar at the Green Room, downtown. The UCSC drinking scene huddled around us like ants on a lump of sugar. I poured libations methodically without discrimination, but Dave employed a different technique. He helped the pretty ladies first, followed by his friends, and lastly, the not-so-pretty ladies before neglecting everybody else, and repeating the process.

As I made my way down the line of thirsty patrons, two toughs forced their way to the bar. We'd known them since elementary school: The Rex Brothers, Hal and Vince. A couple of East Side surf bullies. At some point in the last decade, they'd discovered methamphetamines, which greatly amplified their shitty dispositions. The Rex Brothers wore flat brimmed O'Neil ball caps, black Santa Cruz hoodies with red dots, and across their necks, written in Old English, they sported matching East Side tattoos.

"Two IPA," Hal said to Dave. "Or I kick your ass like back in school."

Dave ignored Hal, and poured a beer for a college girl. Hal grabbed Dave by the collar.

"Knock it off," I yelled as Vince reached over the bar, and sucker punched me in the jaw.

The college scene scattered. I grabbed the baseball bat from behind the counter, and started swinging. When the cops arrived, we assessed the carnage. Dave's eyes were swollen, and he had several lumps on his forehead, but his real concern was the shank to his ribs. Dave got it bad, but not as bad as Hal. Vince fled when the cops arrived, but Hal lay face down in a puddle of blood.

The police looked into the incident, and Ralph, the owner of the Green Room, placed us on leave, pending the outcome of the investigation. Dave didn't mind the time off. He still lived with his parents, and didn't have any real bills, so he didn't have to worry about the financial burden while his wounds healed. I wasn't so fortunate in fiscal matters. I had rent to make on an overpriced one-bedroom apartment, and Elizabeth, my live-in girlfriend, was six months pregnant.

It wasn't the paychecks I missed. It was the nightly tips that paid the bills. With my income on hiatus, I tightened my belt. I cut out buying weed and eating at restaurants. I stayed home and cooked, which wasn't so bad. I considered myself a decent chef.

"Breakfast for dinner again?" Elizabeth said, brushing her long red hair.

"Soft boiled eggs are no easy feat," I said.

"You said the same thing about omelets last night."

The time spent at home, and the lack of income, created stress on our relationship. I could no longer drop a wad of cash on Elizabeth, and she could no longer drop a wad of my cash on the bun in her oven. She was upset. I was hopeful our unfortunate circumstances were temporary.

A few days after the brawl, a detective named Marks knocked on the door. He was as bald as a cue ball with a gut that hinted that he too was pregnant. I invited him in and offered him coffee. He looked around, and determined the place was clean enough to trust a cup.

"You say Hal Rex reached over the bar and grabbed Dave?" He asked and took a sip.

"That's right. I tried to intervene, and that's when Vince punched me."

"What happened next?"

"I grabbed a bat, and jumped over the counter."

"What did you do with the bat?"

"Defended myself."

"Do you remember any specifics?"

"They worked Dave over pretty bad. I tagged Hal, and he went down."

"You're familiar with the Rex Brothers, correct?" Detective Marks asked.

"Yeah," I said. "I've known them since elementary school."

"Have you had issues with them before?"

"They jumped me a few times when we were kids. They're known for kicking ass," I said. "Once, Hal and Vince surfed the Hook and got into a confrontation with a kayaker. They followed him onto land, beat the shit out of the guy, stuffed him back in his canoe, and pushed him over a cliff into the water. Guy broke his neck, and lost the use of his legs. They both ended up doing time. When they got out, they were even meaner. Do you think I need a lawyer?"

"I doubt it'll go to trial," Detective Marks said. "Seems a pretty clear case of self-defense, but I'd steer clear of Vince."

Detective Marks finished his coffee, gave me his card, and left. I was glad no charges were filed against the Green Room or me. That meant I'd be tending bar again soon.

After I was cleared of any wrongdoing, Ralph gave me my shifts back, and life returned to normal. The

UCSC drinkers forgot about the incident and returned to the bar to consume massive quantities of overpriced booze. Dave was on the mend and was expected to return to the Green Room in a few days.

I was covering a Monday afternoon for Nancy. I generally don't work dayshifts or Mondays because business is slow, and the tips aren't there, but Nancy had a family crisis and needed a shift covered. She covered for me when I was on leave, so I owed her.

Besides me, a barfly was the only other person in the Green Room. He sat hunched over his beer nursing it like Florence Nightingale.

"Starting to rain," he said, looking out the window as the front door opened. Vince entered the bar, taking a seat at the counter.

"Sorry about your brother, but you can't be in here," I said.

"I bet you're really sorry about Hal aren't you, Joe?" Vince said. "Where's your boyfriend, Dave?"

"I'm not joking," I said, and put my hand on the bat under the counter. "Get out."

"Or what? You'll crack my skull too?" he said, rising from the stool.

"I feel bad about what happened, but you guys started that shit," I said.

"Elizabeth still a good piece of ass?" Vince asked.

"I'm calling the cops," I said.

"Go ahead," Vince said, exiting the bar, but before he left, he turned, and looked me in the eyes. "You're dead meat."

When my shift ended, I hung around the Green Room for a while, and drank a couple of beers before heading home. Elizabeth was already asleep, so I quietly undressed and crawled into bed, drifting into slumber with my arms wrapped around her swollen belly.

A loud sound woke us late at night. I climbed out of bed, grabbed the Maglite by the nightstand, and walked into the front room. I flicked on the lamp, and looked around. Nothing was out of place except the blinds were slightly askew. I went to fix them, and a small stream of cool air blew against my knuckle. I opened the shades, and saw a small hole in the windowpane surrounded by tiny cracks.

"Fuck," I said.

"What is it?" Elizabeth asked from the bedroom.

I ran my finger along the hole in the glass, stepped back, followed the trajectory, and found another hole in the stucco wall by the bedroom.

I called Detective Marks, but he wasn't available, so I dialed 911. It took a while for a police officer to arrive, so I made a pot of coffee, and we sat at the kitchen table. When an officer finally knocked, he introduced himself as Officer Bailey. I let him in, showed him the bullet hole, and explained the situation. He took a report.

"You think Vince Rex did this?" He asked.

"Yeah," I answered.

"Can you arrest him?" Elizabeth asked.

"No," Officer Bailey said. "There's no proof. It could have been a group of kids firing shots from a moving vehicle."

"Seriously?" I asked.

"Sorry, there's just not much we can do at this time. If you come up with anything else, please let us know."

After Officer Bailey left, we crawled back into bed, but I had a hard time sleeping. Somebody randomly firing a shot through our front window was absurd. I knew it was Vince, and I knew I needed to protect my family. Eventually, I drifted off to sleep. Early the next morning, the phone rang.

"Yeah?"

"Hey Joey, this is Ralph."

"Yeah?"

"I got bad news. Some guy walking his dog this morning found Dave."

"What?"

"He's dead."

"What?"

"He was walking home drunk last night on the tracks. He tripped and hit his head on the rail. At least, that's what the initial reports indicate. I'm sorry to tell you Joey. I know you guys were close."

I hung up the phone and told Elizabeth what had happened. After our initial grieving period, my mind went to work. I thought about Vince Rex telling me I was dead meat, then the bullet hole through the window, and now Dave's death. I didn't know how to proceed, so I called Corey Anderson. He was a buddy of Dave's and mine from school, and now a local defense attorney.

Corey was pretty broken up when I told him about Dave's passing, and then I told him about the situation involving the Rex Brothers. He said he was busy, but he'd move stuff around on his calendar, and make time to meet me for lunch. I met him downtown at a pizzeria. We ordered slices, and sat at a back booth. I told him the long version of the unfortunate recent chain of events as we ate our meal.

"I've dealt with the Rex Brothers before," Corey said, wiping a smudge of marinara off his chin with a napkin. "And I'm not talking about when they used to beat us up in school. They intimidated one of my clients in a smuggling case. After that, my client refused to testify, and the charges against the Rex's were dropped."

"What should I do?" I asked. "I called the police, but they don't give a shit."

"Cops won't do dick until it's too late," Corey said with a mouthful of cheese. "Do you own a gun?"

"No."

"My advice is get one. I've got a snub-nose .38 you can borrow," he said, and threw his wadded napkin onto his paper plate. "I'm due in court in half-an-hour. I have to run. Stop by this evening, and I'll set you up."

I spent the remainder of the day wandering downtown. After sunset, I went home, made French toast for dinner, and then drove to Corey's house. He led me into a walk-in closet at the end of the hall, and opened a box containing multiple pistols.

"Wow, Anderson," I said. "I didn't know you were a gun nut."

"This is nothing. Here we go," Corey said, handing me the .38. "And here's a box of shells."

I thanked him, and went home. Elizabeth sat on the couch watching a sitcom. I didn't want her to see the gun, so I slipped into the bedroom and put it and the ammunition in my nightstand drawer. I joined Elizabeth on the couch for some television, and then went to bed. I had trouble sleeping that night. I kept thinking about the gun. I wasn't sure if it gave me a sense of protection or a sense of vulnerability. One thing was for certain though, every creak in the apartment or grumble from the refrigerator gave me an itchy trigger finger.

The next day, Elizabeth wanted a Polish hot dog with sauerkraut and a coconut snow cone from a hot dog stand up Highway 9. Ben Lomond was a long drive for a hot dog and some shave ice, but I had learned early in the pregnancy to appease my girlfriend's bizarre food cravings. I went out to the car while Elizabeth was in the bathroom, and stashed the gun in the glove compartment. When she finished with her toiletries, we drove through the redwoods up Highway 9.

After lunch, it rained on the way home. A truck tailed us down the winding road. An inch or two separated our bumpers. I got heated, and cussed under my breath when the son of a bitch tapped me. I pulled over at a turnout.

The truck pulled over too, and Vince exited the vehicle. He had a pistol in his hand, so I peeled out, flinging gravel, and sped off. In the rearview mirror, I saw him get back into his truck.

Elizabeth was pale as a ghost. I told her not to worry. She tried calling 911, but there was no reception in the woods. We came to a series of sharp curves, and Vince's truck got back on my bumper. We skidded around a corner, and he rammed us. I lost control and careened off a steep embankment. We flipped over and came to a violent halt against a large redwood. I was knocked unconscious by the impact. When I came to, Elizabeth wasn't in the car.

"Elizabeth?" I yelled. "Elizabeth? Elizabeth? Honey?"

I got out and fell over in excruciating pain. My left shin burned like hell. I dragged myself through the duff and mud until I found Elizabeth. Her breathing was shallow and her pulse was light. I performed CPR, but stopped when a gunshot sounded through the rain. Vince Rex was coming for revenge. I was dead meat.

"You fucked up bad, Joey," Vince yelled from somewhere above. "Now it's time to pay."

"You and your brother caused this," I said, crawling back to the car and removing the .38 from the glove compartment. "And for what? Hal's dead, Dave's dead, and Elizabeth needs medical attention."

"You started this mess when you killed Hal," he yelled and fired another shot. "But it ends here."

Propping myself against the overturned car, I saw Vince descending the embankment in the rain. I took aim and fired. I couldn't tell if I hit him, but the shot halted his forward progress. I fired another shot for safe measure, and waited. I wasn't sure if he'd try to come at us from another angle. I didn't know anything except that Elizabeth needed help.

I waited for Vince, but he never materialized. I looked down at my feet, and saw the bone sticking out of my leg. I felt woozy, so I crawled to Elizabeth and held her tight until darkness enveloped me.

I woke in a hospital bed. Corey sat near me, reading a magazine.

"Elizabeth?"

"She didn't make it," Corey said. "They couldn't save the baby."

His words hurt more than my broken leg. Helplessness and rage flooded every pore of my being. I felt hot and cold at the same time. My eyes shut tight and my teeth clenched. I tried climbing out of bed, but Corey held me down while a nurse injected me with something, and I slipped back into the void.

The day before the funeral, Detective Marks questioned me about the accident, but I didn't mention Vince. Maybe he suspected something, but I doubted it. Detective Marks couldn't find a bee if it stung him in the eye. Besides, whatever punishment the police might have for Vince would be a fucking vacation compared to what I had in store for him.

Rain fell during the funeral. As they lowered Elizabeth and my unborn child six feet under, I stood on crutches, thinking about what little time it takes to have your entire world shattered, burned, and shat upon. I buried my hopes and ambitions with Elizabeth. Only one thing mattered: the same thing that mattered to Vince Rex: revenge. Now it was just a matter of who would serve the dish first.

We walked to Corey's Mazda MX-5—Corey walked—I gimped on crutches. "Dead Meat" was spray-painted across the windshield in red letters.

"Son of a bitch," Corey said, and pulled out his gun. "That prick is here somewhere."

"Good," I said.

141

"You armed?" Corey asked.

"Yeah."

"Then we draw him out. Take a stand," Corey said.

We drove along Soquel Avenue. I kept looking back, but I didn't see a tail. We passed through Capitola, and down into Soquel. Corey took a left on Old San Jose Road, and we ascended the curvy thruway. After several minutes of winding turns, I looked back, and saw Vince's truck.

"Bingo," I said. "Now what?"

"Up the road it winds along a steep cliff," Corey said. "We get a little distance from this prick, park around a sharp turn, and as he comes into view, we end this shit."

Vince was a dog on the hunt, but we were wolves, leading the hunter astray. As far as I was concerned, Vince was the dead meat. We climbed a steep grade through redwood groves. Corey mashed the gas. Vince tried to keep pace, but Corey's sports car out performed Vince's truck. As we rounded a bend, the trees ended, and a sheer cliff loomed. Giant floating gray warship clouds filled an angry sky. Hundreds of feet below, dark green treetops blurred together.

Corey pulled onto a small muddy turnout, and positioned the car sideways. We exited the vehicle, and drew our guns. Corey used the roof to steady his aim. I leaned against the hood, using it as a crutch. Through the rain, Vince's truck approached. I took a deep breath, and as my enemy came into view, we opened fire. Bullet holes riddled the windshield. The truck veered and crashed into Corey's car. I lunged out of harm's way into the mud just before the thunderous impact.

"Corey?" I yelled as I picked myself up.

I hopped on one foot to the cab of the truck with my gun in hand. Vince was hunched over the wheel. I hopped to the other side of the wreck, and found Corey's head smashed under the rear wheel in a pool of blood. I hopped back to Vince's truck, and opened the driver's side door.

"Die," he said and shot me in the neck.

I fell in the mud holding my throat. Large raindrops carpet-bombed the area. I staggered to my feet, blood pouring down my shirt. Another shot rang out, hitting me in the chest. I felt a horrible burning pain, but stayed upright. I raised my gun, and shot Vince in the side. He violently flailed into the passenger seat. I climbed in. Vince gasped for air. I turned over the engine several times until the ignition caught, and the truck roared to life.

Revenge had ground us both into bloody sausage. My chest heaved as I backed away from Corey's wrecked sport's car. Through the pain, a warming peaceful feeling enveloped me. The gray warship clouds thundered overhead. I mashed down on the gas pedal, and hurled our dead meat off the cliff toward the dark green blur of trees below.

The Con after the Storm

The storm knocked out the neighborhood's power. It was still raining the next day as Eddie and I drove through the old folk's trailer park. Tree branches littered front yards, and the gutters overflowed with runoff and debris. The elderly residence sat under eaves on their front porches, waiting for the restoration of electricity. At the last trailer on the block, an old lady sat alone in a rocking chair, knitting a quilt.

"Her," Eddie said.

I turned the corner and parked the van.

I first met Eddie in Juvenile Hall. He was my cellmate. Like me, his youth was spent in abusive foster homes. Eddie landed in Juvie as a result of his violent tendencies. I gained residency in the Hall for borrowing other kid's video game consoles. I didn't think it was a problem, but apparently appropriating something from a locked house with nobody home was a no-no.

Eddie was a massive hulking giant with an exceptionally small head, a limp, and a harelip. The other kids in the Hall mocked him obsessively about his large stature, tiny head and goofy walk until he started cracking skulls. After that, nobody messed with him.

144

I was an average kid of normal height and build, with one exception–a shock of white hair blazed across the left side of my black locks. Everybody called me Skunk and ostracized me, but it wasn't until puberty that I really attained freak status.

Most kids have acne in adolescence, but one morning, I woke up, and oozing red boils had colonized the entire surface of my face. Real estate was especially desirable on my nose. My carbuncular appearance made me the ridicule of every schoolyard I hallowed. In Juvie, Eddie stuck up for me. If my bubbly face offended some kid, Eddie offended the kid's face with his fists. After Juvenile Hall, the plundering wens disappeared as mysteriously as they had arrived, leaving my head a pockmarked moon.

Our socially unacceptable physical appearances, and our similar experiences growing up in shitty foster homes, initially bonded us while doing time together, but it was grifting that solidified our camaraderie. Released from incarceration around the same time, we split the rent on a dumpy apartment. Stealing video game cartridges from Walmart, and hocking them at the used videogame stores was our initial source of income. We made rent with this line of work for several months until the venture ceased being lucrative. Our next endeavor entailed rolling drunks after the bars let out, and again our enterprise kept a roof overhead until Eddie got a little too rough with a drunkard one night, and shattered the poor bastard's teeth with a ball-peen hammer.

It was a rotten thing to do, but I figured nobody cared enough about an alky's dental work to cause a stink. I was wrong. The incident made the evening news. They even broadcast sketches of the suspects. The profiles looked nothing like us. I don't know how you screw that up because a haggard skunk and a giant with a baby's head are sights you don't soon forget. I attribute the misidentification to luck, but regardless of our good fortune, the gig was up, and we were forced to seek other means of gainful employment.

We sat in the van, eating a cold pizza. I didn't like the look in Eddie's eye, and I certainly didn't like what he'd done to the last old lady we'd marked. I meant to have a chat with him, but I never got around to it. I finished my half of the pie, and pulled a dark work cap low over my brow, obscuring my hair and face. I exited the van into the rain, wearing a denim shirt and khaki pants with a flashlight in my pocket. Eddie stayed put, washing his pizza down with a two-liter bottle of Pepsi. When I reached the old lady's porch, the rocking chair was empty.

"Who's there?" an old woman's voice asked from within after I knocked on the front door.

"Electric company," I said.

"Power's been out all day," the voice replied, and the door cracked as much as the chain allowed. "There was a loud crash last night, and the lights went out."

"Lines down all over town," I said. "I'm here to restore your juice. Can I come in?"

"You're with the electric company?"

"Yes," I said. "We're going door to door."

"I don't know," the voice hesitated.

"It'll be several days to a week before we can get you back on the grid if you miss this appointment."

"Okay," the warbling voice said, and the door opened.

I switched on my flashlight, and entered the darkened living room. A couch and a table stacked with quilts occupied the space. There was also a recliner, and an old television set. Embroidered kitsch hung on the walls, and a framed certificate of sobriety. A musty smell lingered in the air.

"Where's the breaker panel?" I asked, and the old woman led me down the hall to a closet.

The tiny walk-in was filled with quilts. Various intricate patterns and colors adorned the folded blankets. She removed a stack, revealing a metal box in the wall. I pointed my light at the breaker switches, and rubbed my stubbly chin.

"I'll have your lights on in no time."

"Oh good," she said.

"It's an easy fix, but it requires a fifty-dollar down payment."

"Fifty dollars," she said, wrinkling her brow and wringing her hands.

"Standard procedure."

"Hold on," she said, and disappeared into the bedroom. I stood still, listening to a drawer open and close. She returned with a fifty-dollar bill. I stuffed Grant into my pocket, and flipped the breakers on and off.

"Where's your husband?" I asked.

"Passed away," she said.

"Sorry to hear that. I left my voltmeter in the truck. I need it to check your current. Be right back."

Normally, I'd just take the money and move on to the next sucker, but old people don't trust banks. They tend to keep their savings squirreled away in their homes. Not to mention, I didn't even know what a voltmeter was, or how to use one, but I sounded like I did.

"How'd it go?" Eddie asked as I climbed into the van.

"As expected," I said, and flashed the fifty-dollar bill. "She's alone, and keeps her money hidden in her bedroom."

"Dentures?" Eddie asked.

"Let's go," I said, ignoring the question. "She thinks I went to get a tool."

I grabbed my loaded snub-nosed .38 from the glove compartment and put it in my pocket. I wasn't expecting trouble, but I wasn't taking chances either. We exited the van, and made our way through the rain. I wished Eddie would at least try not to limp. If somebody saw us, and had to give our descriptions to the authorities, a giant with a hitch substantially drained the pool of suspects.

The door was still unlocked, so we switched on our flashlights, and entered the living room. I tried to tell the old lady I brought along a coworker, but before I could say anything, Eddie knocked her to the floor.

Eddie was never really in it for the money. He enjoyed making people suffer. I came to this realization back when we rolled drunks. My interest was strictly financial, but Eddie delighted in blackening an eye, breaking a bone, or powdering some poor bastard's teeth. Fortunately, most old ladies we conned were toothless, but regardless, I needed to rein Eddie in before we lost another form of employment.

"Lighten up," I said. "She's frangible."

"Grab the dough," Eddie barked.

I went into the old lady's bedroom, and pointed my flashlight at an oak dresser, removing drawers, and turning them upside down. The top ones contained clothes, and the bottom ones were filled with more colorful quilts. I rifled through everything, but found no money. I was about to check under the bed when I heard Eddie swearing.

"What's wrong?" I asked, running back into the living room.

"She's got an emergency alert device around her neck," he said. "I saw her push the button. We better dip before the cops show."

"We're safe," I said. "The power's out. She can't notify anybody."

"I don't like it," Eddie said, and removed the electronic pendant from her neck. "You get the money?"

"I'm still looking," I said, and returned to the bedroom.

I tore apart the bed, and searched under the frame, finding more quilts. I pointed the flashlight at a nightstand, and removed the drawer. I discovered a leather satchel, opened it, and hit the jackpot, locating several thick bundles of cash. I snatched the money, stashing it in my pockets as something else inside the bag caught my eye.

I trained my flashlight on an old yellowing photograph. The image was of a young boy. He looked about three years old. He had a toy ball in one hand and a water pistol in the other, and Band-Aids taped to both knees. A small streak of white hair marked the left side of his head.

I paid special attention to the boy's facial features. His smiling eyes were completely ignorant of the horrors that lay ahead. I ran my fingers over my scarred visage, gazing at the child's smooth complexion until a mournful sound drew my attention away from the picture.

I returned to the living room, and pointed my flashlight at Eddie. He stood over the old lady with his pants around his ankles.

"Give me a minute," he said, looking back with a sneer.

The old lady was on the floor, crying. I drew my .38, and shot Eddie in the back of his tiny head. His massive body crumpled, and blood gushed from the wound.

I pointed the flashlight at the old lady.

"Don't hurt me," she said.

I pocketed the gun, turned the flashlight onto my face, removed my ball cap, and revealed the shock of white hair against my blackened coiffure.

"Skunky-Poo?" She asked in bewilderment.

I helped her to her feet as the front door opened, and a police officer with a drawn service revolver ordered me to put up my hands and get down on the ground. I lay on the floor, realizing the crucial mistake I'd made: the emergency alert device ran on batteries.

I had hoped to beat the rap on those home invasions, but fingerprints don't lie. Fortunately, I wasn't charged with Eddie's murder, or I'd be facing twenty-five to life. The judge at my trial deemed it self-defense. My return to incarceration has been hard, especially without Eddie there to protect me, but I can't complain. It could be worse. At least I have one of mom's hand stitched quilts to keep me warm at night in my prison cell.

Sour Sixteen

The day I turned sixteen, I wanted to get hammered. My mom was out of town with her piece of shit boyfriend, so I had the trailer to myself. I called Jimmy to see if he wanted to hangout, and get fucked up. Jimmy was a hippy who always had weed. When he arrived, Jimmy was wearing a tie-dyed Jerry Garcia t-shirt, but he was out of weed. He said we could scrape his pipe. That didn't sound too fucking good, so I took the ten dollars my mom left me for Burger King, and we walked to the bus stop across the street from Dave's Liquors.

Early that morning, before my mom and her worthless dickhead boyfriend got out of bed, I swiped half a pack of Marlboro's from shithead's truck. I didn't feel bad about it either because that prick never does anything for me except give me a ration of shit. I mean it was my fucking sixteenth birthday, and he didn't even give a fuck.

Me and Jimmy smoked at the bus stop while arguing about music.

"Tool kicks the Grateful Dead's ass."

"It's like apples and oranges, man. They both have their place."

Mostly, it was square-ass dick-weeds coming and going from Dave's. They all either looked like narcs or pussies, so we waited. It was getting late, and the smokes were getting low, and I was getting super impatient when I saw just the right motherfucker - a dirty-ass bum with a rotten beard pushing a shopping cart filled with trash through Dave's parking lot.

"Hey," I said, crossing the street.

"I didn't do nothin'," he said, startled.

His eyes swirled and he clawed at his greasy beard with his blackened fingernails.

"Nobody said you did."

"Wha you want?"

"Would you do me a favor?" I asked, holding out the ten spot. "Can you buy me a 12 pack of Bud?"

"Can't leave my cans," he said.

"I'll keep an eye on them for you."

He thought about it for a moment, all the while scratching that dirty beard with his rotten pickles until he agreed, but not before he made me promise not to snatch any of his disgusting aluminum. I swore on my father's grave I'd keep his garbage safe.

He took the ten, and limped into the liquor store.

Nervously, I smoked and waited in the parking lot. It felt like an eternity. What the fuck was he doing in there? How goddamn hard was it to buy some fucking beer?

Through the large glass windows, I watched the troll wandering the aisles, talking to himself, until he finally grabbed a twelver. At the counter, he tried to pay, but the clerk shook his head and pointed towards the door. They started arguing. The bum got hella pissed, and I almost shit my pants when he shanked the clerk in the neck with a blade. A geyser of blood erupted from the clerk's wound as the bum fled with the beer.

"Holy fucking shit," I said as the bum handed me the bloody Bud. "What'd you do that for?"

"Self-defense," he said, just before his head exploded.

The bum toppled over his shopping cart, spilling his aluminum cans and brains onto the pavement. The clerk stood in the doorway, blood squirting from his neck, holding up a big ass .45. He pointed the piece at me, so I ditched the beer, and raised my hands to the sky. I thought I was a motherfucking goner for sure, but instead the dying clerk sagged to his knees, and keeled over onto his face.

Me and Jimmy hauled ass back to the trailer park, shitting bricks the entire way. In the distance, sirens howled like hellhounds.

"Fuck, dude," I said to Jimmy as I opened the front door. "I really wish you had some fucking weed right about now."

"I wish you hadn't ditched the beer," Jimmy said. "Your fingerprints are all over that 12 pack."

"Fuck," I said, and turned on the light.

"Surprise," my mom and her worthless dickhead boyfriend yelled from the living room, holding a store-bought cake. "Happy birthday."

Bad Batch

I undo my seatbelt, and find Zack lying motionless outside the twisted truck, his head on backwards. The skin on his face crawls, but no breath escapes his lips. Blood and sparkling lights drip out of his nose.

The cliff is too sheer to climb back up to the road, but a trail leads down into the glinting mist. Trees close in around me. I lose my balance, flinching through a massive spider web, and tumble into a thorny bush. Branches claw my arms and face as I return to the trail, and discover ticks peppering my arms. A quick search of my body reveals another bloodsucker in my bellybutton. I pinch the little bastard out with a bad case of the shivers.

The path leads to a creek. Yellow eyes loom in the surrounding wilderness as I follow the water. Flapping butterfly wings sparkle trails of fairy dust through the air. A pungent and familiar smell fills my nostrils. A cursory glance confirms my suspicion: an illegal grow operation.

"Hands up," a man demands with a rifle trained at me.

The barrel of the gun slithers like a snake. The man wears a clown mask. The most majestic unicorn bounds between us. I take the opportunity to flee. Bullets ping off surrounding rocks. A quick glance over my shoulder reveals several armed clowns in hot pursuit.

Following the stream, I scramble over boulders and branches until the creek plummets over a thousand-foot cliff. Frantically, I search for safe passage down the precipice, but find none as the armed clowns approach. Bullets whiz by. I reach into my pocket and remove the vial, dumping its contents on my tongue.

"Kiss my ass, motherfuckers," I yell as wings shoot out of my back, and I bound off the cliff into the swirling rainbow void.

Finder's Fee

"You in a hurry or somethin'?" I ask Charlie from my golf cart.

We get all kinds of trash at Lucho's dump, and then there's the refuse. It's hard work, keeping track of who's dropping off and who's picking through. Lucho don't allow no pickers. He'd shit can my fat ass in an abnormal heart beat if he knew the grease on my palm.

"N-no, Robin," Charlie says, and pushes his thick black framed glasses held together by wire back up his nose.

Picking here works for Charlie because he always got grease for my palm and a stogie for my yap.

"You wasn't letting out without approval?" I ask, and shift my gnawed cigar butt from one corner of my mouth to the other.

I manage the dry pit and hustle pickers on the sly. It don't pay as much as the wet pit, but there ain't enough gold in hell for me to work that slop hole. It ain't the rotting beef smell or the circling seagulls dropping crap bombs neither. I got a cousin, JoJo, on the soggy end says the wet racket's a lot meaner: body disposal for the mob.

"N-no, Robin," Charlie says.

"What you got?"

Charlie swipes his messy bangs out of his face. A long cardboard tube protrudes from his dirty tote bag. He pushes it to the side, and removes some gewgaw from the sack.

"H-here, Robin. I-I pulled a couple old action figures. D-do you remember H-He-Man and the Masters of the Universe?"

"Nah."

"Th-this is Skeletor and Beastman."

"Worth anything?"

"I-I might catch a few bucks for 'em at the swap meet. If-if they clean up."

"What else?" I ask, and rap Charlie in the puss.

"Th-this," he stutters, and hands me an old rusty broken pocket watch. "Th-this might fetch a pretty-pretty penny."

"Probably crap," I say, looking it over, and putting it in my pocket.

"Y-you never know."

"That it?"

"Y-yes," Charlie says, and starts walking toward the gate, but there's something peculiar about his stride—something I don't like in his limp.

I drive my golf cart past him, and park in front of the exit.

"Wh-what is it, Robin?" He asks. "D-do you want Skeletor too?"

"You in an awful big hurry," I say, looking him over. "What's in the tube?"

"Oh, th-that," Charlie says as if he forgot to mention it. "J-just some paper."

"Gimme."

Charlie sighs, and hands me the tube. I take off the top, remove and unfurl the scroll. It's a two-tone yellow and black movie poster, browning at the edges. Behind a

157

stupid staring robot's all these shafts of light and windowless skyscrapers. The bottom says, Ein Film Von Fritz Lang, and the top says *Metropolis*.

"The hell is this?" I ask.

"N-nothing," Charlie says. "Prob-probably just a copy—n-not worth the paper it's printed on."

"Looks old," I say scratching my nuts. "Let's consult the Google."

I search "Metropolis movie poster" on my cracked phone as Charlie deflates like a tire. A site pops up called "The 10 Most Expensive Film Posters—in Pictures."

"Beef jerky Jesus," I say.

"It-it's mine," Charlie says. "G-give it back. I-I'll tell Lucho if you don't."

"Have a seat," I say. "Let's discuss."

Charlie reluctantly climbs aboard my golf cart, and I step on the gas.

Can't have Charlie hocking no poster from my pit for half a rock. Word'd get out for sure. Can't have him diming to Lucho on me neither. Don't want to get hit by no shit can. Good thing Cousin JoJo owes me one. Paper and flesh don't last long under all that rotten lettuce.

"Things is gonna work out just fine," I say to Charlie, and shift my gnawed cigar butt from one corner of my mouth to the other as seagull crap starts falling out the sky.

The Turkey

I won my last two fights. One more and I get my first turkey. A turkey means better billing, better fights, and better money. Better money means making rent, providing for my family, and it means I don't work for the wrong people no more. I've seen these guys make the devil blush deep in the desert, and it haunts me. I got to get out. I got to get my little brother out too. I introduced him to the life, and now he's some kind of lackey for these men.

I crushed my last two opponents. I choked out Edwards, and broke Sprat's jaw. The next guy I fight's Randal James, and I've put in the work: brutal camp, supplements, ate clean, cycled my PEDS. He doesn't stand a chance. I'll grind him into hamburger meat.

Before the fight my employers convince me to take a dive. It breaks my heart, but these aren't the type of people you fuck with. I say bye-bye to my turkey, and get in the cage with James. We collide like two stags fighting over Bambi's mom. I'm not supposed to win, but that don't mean I can't bust him up a little. Got to make it look good, like this chump's whooped before he knocks me out.

In the third round, I'm supposed to get tagged by a big shot and go down. James kicks me in the liver, followed by a hook to the ear. I should drop, but instead I stick out a jab. I touch him square on the chin, and he melts like butter. His feet find no perch, and his face splatters on the mat.

"Night, night," I say, and drop a savage sledgehammer on his head.

Backstage, my teammates and trainers celebrate my win, my first turkey, and I should celebrate too, but I'm in trouble, so I don't enjoy the moment. I walk to my car outside the arena, and a man pokes a pistol into my spine. Two more men flank my sides, directing me toward a limousine.

We sit in the back. I'm sandwiched between the thugs. The third man sits adjacent, leveling the gun at me.

"Congrats on your turkey," he says.

I complain about James' glass jaw, but they just laugh. At best, I'm hoping for a pistol-whipping, but I know we've been driving long enough to do some serious middle of the desert bullshit.

The limo pulls over, and my life flashes before my eyes. Each second becomes precious. I go soft, sobbing and begging as I'm forced from the car. This invokes their derision, so I switch gears and fight for my life, but I get smacked on the back of the head by a pistol, and collapse into a heap of twinkling purple stars.

I'm dragged to my feet. A shovel's placed in my hands. It takes some persuading, but I dig my own grave. When the hole's deep enough, they take the shovel away, and kick me to my knees. A million thoughts explode in my mind. I feel the barrel of the gun against the back of my head. I take in a deep breath, and then: bang!

My executioner topples into my grave. Two more explosions ring out, and the other two men fall to the ground with blood pouring from their heads.

"You're not the only one got a turkey tonight," my little brother says, holding a pistol. "They probably shouldn't have made me the driver on this job."

"Thanks," I say, rising to my feet. "But we're as good as dead now."

"I wouldn't worry about it. You've got more important things on your plate," my little brother says, tossing me the shovel. "Like one more win, and you get your first hambone."

The Rex

Kate had something to tell me, but she wouldn't say it over the phone. I knew it wouldn't be good news, so I started scheming ways to leave work. Cutting out early would have been doable except for the weather. Aging movie patrons descended upon the cinema like rats at the first sign of a plague as sheets of rain came down, crushing any hopes of an early departure. To make matters worse, Michael, the general manager, conveniently complained of a horrible stomach pain, and disappeared into the bathroom, leaving me to cover the box and the floor by my lonesome.

A guy, in a cap twisted backwards and a backpack slung over his shoulder, stepped to the window.

"What's playing?" He asked, several front teeth missing.

"The synopsis is taped to the window."

"Any good?"

"Buy a ticket, and find out."

"Let me ask you a question," he said. "Deer, cow and horse all eat grass, but deer shits pellets, cow shits a patty, and horse shits a clump of grass. Why do you suppose that is?"

"I don't know," I said.

"Exactly. You don't know shit," he said, putting a free admittance token through the window before entering the theater.

"That roach coach did a number on me. I'll be back later to help close," Michael said, exiting the bathroom and colliding with shoeless Dave The Bum. "Where's your ticket?"

"Come on, man," Dave The Bum said. "It's raining."

"Buy a ticket or get out," Michael demanded, leading him outside. "Next time you sneak in, I call the cops."

When the last ticket was torn, I started the film. I'm a projectionist, but with the advent of the digital projector, a one–armed, one-fingered, one-balled chimpanzee could run a show. There was no more cutting, splicing, and looping film. Starting a movie was now about as complicated as turning on a flat screen television.

After pushing play, I returned to the lobby for closing duties, alone. Wasn't the first time; wouldn't be the last. Just meant I had to hustle if I wanted to get home to Kate at a reasonable hour.

Dave The Bum knocked on the box window. Soaking wet, he held his hands in supplication. "Please," formed on his lips. I should have ignored him, but instead, I unlocked the front door.

"Thanks," he said in a gravelly, fried voice as I went back to my closing duties. "Your mama raised you right."

"That way," I said, pointing to the theater.

"Spare some popcorn?" he asked.

Ignoring his question, I dumped the night's un-purchased popcorn into the trash, and wiped down the kettle.

I was opening a plastic bag of large soda cups with my box cutter when several patrons came out of the auditorium complaining about the lack of picture on the screen. The best way to fix a malfunctioning digital projector is to shut it all the way down to the breaker. After killing the power, I let the machine reboot. When everything was a go, I started the film again. Ninety-nine percent of the time a reboot fixed the problem, but this issue fell into the one percentile, and again no picture appeared on the screen. I flipped on the house lights and strolled into the auditorium. At the foot of the little stage at the base of the screen, I turned around and faced the ageing patrons.

A chorus of boos greeted my announcement that the late show was cancelled due to technical difficulties. As I refunded costumers in the lobby, an alarm screeched from the auditorium. Somebody had exited out the side door. Ever since that asshole shot up that Colorado movie theater, emergency exits in cinemas required alarms. After resetting the alarm, I locked the front door when the last grumpy old man received the last refund.

As I continued my closing duties, somebody knocked on the box window. I was about to tell Dave The Bum to fuck off, but when I looked up, it was Missing Teeth pressing his face against the glass.

"Left my backpack in the theater. Let me back in."

Protocol dictated that after locking the theater's doors, re-admittance was not allowed. Normally, I would have forgone protocol, and opened the door, but this guy was an asshole. Plus, I didn't have time to dick around, looking for some bullshit. I needed to get home to Kate.

"Can't help you," I said.

Missing Teeth banged and kicked on the glass. Taking out my phone, I dialed 911, but didn't hit send, and put the screen up to the glass, so he could see my intentions. Missing Teeth kicked the door one last time, and disappeared into the rain.

Alone in the theater at night was always creepy. As I walked the aisles to make sure nobody was still in the auditoriums, I got the feeling somebody else was present. People liked to say the Rex was haunted, but I'd never seen a ghost. Didn't see Missing Teeth's backpack either.

After finishing my closing duties, I rolled my bicycle out the storage closet and wheeled it into the lobby just as the night janitor unlocked the front door.

"Hola," Ricardo said. "A man outside wants in. I say no. He gets mad. You want him in?"

"No."

"You ride your bike home?"

"Yeah."

"Careful. It's wet. Don't slip," Ricardo said, strapping on a backpack vacuum, and sucking popcorn up off the lobby floor.

The theater's marquee reflected hazy neon colors off the rain puddles. I pedaled toward the river path, noticing a car behind me. I moved right, but the automobile didn't pass. I looked back: no headlights. Hopping the curb, I cut through an apartment complex. Tires screamed around the corner as I reached the next street.

If I made the river, the car couldn't follow me onto the levy. Cranking pedals through a red light, I narrowly avoided an oncoming pickup truck, bolted through a parking lot, and climbed a short, steep embankment.

An old brown Cadillac without headlights idled in the parking lot below. Reaching into my pocket, I dialed 911 on my phone, but the battery was dead. Above the roaring river, the Cadillac's engine revved. Tires squealed and the car climbed the embankment. I chucked my bike, and fumbled into the bushes.

A car door slammed, and something whizzed by my head, followed by the cracking boom of a gunshot. The shadow of a figure neared. Normally, I would have chosen flight in this situation, but with a rain-swollen river at my back, and a man with a gun approaching, I opted for fight. During the struggle, the man dropped the gun, and we tumbled into the river's shallows. Hands tightened around my neck, holding my face underwater. Tiny purple stars twinkled in my vision, and my lungs burned. I reached into my pocket, and blindly thrust the box cutter at my attacker.

The hands released from my throat, and I raised my head out of the water with a horrible cough. Something gurgled nearby as I scrambled onto the river path. A man in a shiny gray suit smoked a cigarette against the Cadillac. As I approached, he jumped into the car, and drove down the embankment.

"Get your ass on the ground," somebody demanded behind me. "Police."

I lay prone on the ground as hands patted me down.

"Where's the gun? I heard a shot," a plain clothed police officer said with a pistol trained at my face.

I told him about the Cadillac, the dark figure with the gun, and the fight that ended with me possibly slashing my assailant. The cop said his name was Detective Banks, and that he was nearby, writing a report in an unmarked police car when he heard the gunshot. He holstered his revolver, and told me to stay where I was while he went down to the river to investigate. In a few minutes, he returned.

"Nobody's down there, but I found a gun," Detective Banks said, wiping blood from his hand onto his pants. "Let's head to the station for your statement."

On the drive, police lights filled the Rex's courtyard.

"Pull over," I said.

"Somebody bludgeoned Ricardo to death," Michael said as Banks and I entered the lobby.

Paramedics wheeled Ricardo out on a stretcher under a white blanket. Banks told me to get back into the car, and we drove past the police department. After several blocks, Banks parked in a dark alley behind a Cadillac.

"Where's the backpack?" He asked.

"I don't know."

"Make this easy on yourself. Tell me."

"I would if I could."

"Fair enough," Banks said. "Out you go."

A dome light switched on in the Cadillac as a man in a gray sharkskin suit got out of the car and approached.

"Here's your partner's gun," Banks said. "Kid says he doesn't have the money. No more fucking messes like that bastard in the theater. Nobody ever finds this body, we clear?"

I sat in the backseat next to Sharkskin as the Cadillac rolled downtown. The driver wore a ball cap twisted backwards. Looking over his shoulder at me, Missing Teeth smiled, revealing a blood-encrusted bandage wrapped around his throat before returning his attention back to the road.

"Where's it at?" Sharkskin asked.

"Don't know," I said, and he jabbed me in the ribs with a screwdriver.

I couldn't tell if it was Philips or flat head, but it hurt like hell.

"My associate left a backpack filled with cash in your theater," Sharkskin said, putting the screwdriver blade up my nostril. "I just unscrewed your janitor looking for it, but he didn't have my money. So that leaves you, night manager. Now I want your complete attention. You have until dawn to return what's mine. Do we understand each other? Call me when you have it."

He removed the screwdriver from my nose, and put a burner phone in my hand.

"Don't try cutting out neither. Remember, the pigs are in our pocket. We know where you live too. We know you're shacking up with a redhead named Kate.

Hate for something to happen to her. You have until sunrise."

The Cadillac pulled to the curb in front of an Irish Pub. Sharkskin opened the door and pushed me onto the sidewalk. An old lady asked if I was okay as the Cadillac pulled away. Unable to answer, I walked toward the Rex, holding my damaged ribs, and wiping blood from my nose onto my shirt. It hurt to breath, hurt to step, and it hurt to move, but I kept on. What else could I do? Lie down and die. That was already happening tomorrow.

I unlocked the glass door, walked around the caution tape into the theatre, and turned on the lights. Searching down every row, I checked between and under each seat, hoping to find the backpack. My search yielded nothing. I sat down in the front row.

The small stage under the screen was covered in a thin layer of dust, except for a line of footprints. Not shoe prints, but actual left and right, heal, ball and toe prints. I followed the tracks to the edge of the screen, and pulled back the curtain, revealing old busted seats and a ratty rug. Backstage functioned as a storage area for stuff we didn't know what to do with, but there was also something else present: trash. Fast food wrappers and empty liquor bottles scattered across the floor. A tattered blanket and piles of filthy clothes littered the back corner.

Before leaving the theater, I heard a noise. At the top of the stairs next to the projection booth, a sliver of light showed under the manager's office.

"Hi, Ed," Michael said when I opened the door.

"Still here?" I asked, noticing the gun on the desk.

"Did you know the Rex is for sale? I was trying to borrow the cash to cover the down. The transaction was supposed to take place tonight after the late show. I left early with an upset stomach, figuring I'd return in time to meet with the lenders. I didn't count on the projector shitting the bed, and you closing early."

"Is one of these lenders missing teeth, and does the other wear a sharkskin suit?"

"I never got the money," Michael said, picking up the gun, and pointing it at me. "But they don't care. They say if I don't pay them back, I'll join Ricardo."

"I'm on that list too," I said.

"If Ricardo didn't find the money, that leaves only you. If you'd have just let the guy back in to grab his backpack, we wouldn't be in this mess."

"It wouldn't have mattered if I let him back in," I said. "The backpack was already gone."

"Who took it?"

"Dave The Bum."

"If that's true, I'm already dead," Michael said, putting the gun back on the table.

On my way out, a gunshot reverberated throughout the theater. Cautiously, I made my way back into the manager's office. Michael sat in his chair with the gun on his lap. His brains splattered against the *Metropolis* movie poster on the wall behind him.

Outside, I puked in a planter box before walking to the river path. Homeless encampments peppered the shore.

"What you want?" A haggard and stubbly face asked under the dim glow of a lighter.

"Looking for Dave The Bum?"

"Why?"

"Twenty bucks if you don't ask questions."

"Happy Know Dave."

The homeless man beckoned me to follow before the lighter went out. We crept through tall grass and bushes until we came to another encampment.

"Happy, you here?" The bum asked, and a flashlight illuminated a young man with a red ponytail.

"Mom?" Happy asked.

"Nah, it's Hustle. Got a dude here want to know where Bummy Dave at."

"Mom?"

"He thinks everybody his dead mom," Hustle said. "Yeah, Happy. Your momma need to know where Dave at."

"He got a room at the Dreamtime Inn."

The Dreamtime Inn was a tourist hotel in the Flats. Hotels abounded in this low income area due to their proximity to the boardwalk. I departed from Hustle and twenty dollars, and walked to the 7-Eleven across the street from the Dreamtime Inn.

Through the convenient store's doors, a flux of prostitutes and junkies came and went. Leaning against a wall in the shadows, I was about to call it quits, head home, and spend what little time I had left with Kate when Dave The Bum crossed the street, holding hands with a corpulent woman. He was still barefoot, and she wore daisy dukes and a midriff. As they entered the 7-Eleven, I made the call.

An hour later, Missing Teeth sat in the front seat of the Cadillac with a clean bandage taped to his neck. I sat in the back with Sharkskin as he impatiently loosened and tightened the screws to the door's side paneling with his screwdriver.

"What do you say?" Sharkskin asked Missing Teeth. "Should I take this kid apart and see how full of shit he is?"

Missing Teeth cracked a grin as Dave The Bum staggered from the Dreamtime Inn toward the 7-Eleven.

"There," I said, and Sharkskin hopped out the car.

"Pardon me, pal. How do I get to the boardwalk?" Sharkskin asked, waving at Dave The Bum.

"Valley's back that way," Dave said.

Sharkskin grabbed the bum by the scruff, and flung him into the backseat.

"This really the guy has our skrill?" Sharkskin asked.

"Ain't got shit," Dave The Bum said, but his denial was met with a screwdriver to the ribs.

Dave The Bum doubled over, throwing up on the floorboard.

"For the past few nights, Dave The Bum's been squatting behind the movie screen at the Rex after the late show gets out," I said. "Last night, he planned to do the same to get out of the rain, but when the picture went out on the projector, he found your backpack full of cash in the seats, and headed out the emergency exit for the comfort of the Dreamtime Inn."

Sharkskin took Dave's hotel key from the bum's pant pocket as Missing Teeth drove us across the street.

"Better have my money, or I unscrew your balls," Sharkskin said, forcing Dave from the car.

Dave's room smelled like burnt wire as we entered. Dave's lady sat naked on the bed, lighting a glass crack pipe. The backpack lay on the floor with hundred-dollar bills spilling out the side. She coughed great clouds of foul-smelling smoke, and grabbed a handgun from the nightstand. Before Missing Teeth could draw his weapon, he took a bullet to the gut, and dropped like a sack of wet shit. Sharkskin shielded himself with Dave as the woman unloaded the handgun into the bum's body.

"Got a little smudge here," Sharkskin said, tossing Dave's riddled body aside and looking at his lapel.

A dime-sized spot of blood grew into a silver dollar. Sharkskin tried wiping away the stain before collapsing to the ground.

"You want a hit?" The woman asked, grabbing the crack pipe.

"I'm good," I said, backing away from the carnage.

She took another hit from the crack pipe, and disappeared into the bathroom.

Out on the street, the prostitutes and junkies scuttled to and fro in front of the 7-Eleven. The dawn's first light reflected off the night's rain puddles. Doubling my step, I made my way home along the river path.

In the apartment's courtyard, the Cadillac idled. The driver side door was open, but nobody was behind the wheel. A trail of watery blood led to my apartment. Inside, I found Missing Teeth sitting on my couch in a pool of his own gore.

"Came her to kill your girl before I bleed out," Missing Teeth said with a weak gurgle.

"Who doesn't know shit now," I said, kneeling beside Kate, and kissing her cold purple lips. "So dear, what is it you wanted to tell me?"

Snaked

We were gathering wood at an undisclosed location deep in the mountains when I heard a rattling in the pile. I dropped the wood in my arms and drew my gun.

"Don't shoot," Murray said.

"I'm not getting bit way the fuck out in the middle of nowhere," I said.

"Tell the doctor."

I holstered my gun and walked to the little cabin. It was a real dumpy piece of shit–one tiny bedroom and one tiny kitchen/living room. There was electricity but no indoor plumbing. Dr. Cross sat at a small table, reading a medical journal.

"No wood?" He asked.

"Rattler in the stack."

His eyes lit up, and he grabbed a long metal rod with a hook at the end. At the woodpile, the doctor poked the pole into various crevices until the viper hissed and struck at the rod. The serpent wrapped around the end of the pole, and Dr. Cross removed it from the stack. Pinching the snake below the head, he held it before me.

"Good size," he said.

"Keep it away," I said, backing up.

"Don't be a little girl," Murray said with a laugh.

Under the guise of providing protection, I was hired to relieve Murray of his sentinel duties, and put an end to the good doctor's relationship with my employer. The organization I worked for had retained Dr. Cross for his uncanny ability to dissolve flesh and bone. For a time, this symbiotic relationship proved productive for both sides in that my employer murdered for money, and Dr. Cross received an unlimited supply of cadavers for his bizarre experiments. As of late, the doctor's notoriety had sky-rocketed, mostly in the form of making the FBI's top ten most wanted list, and thus my employer no longer wished to maintain ties with the underground M.D.

Holding the snake, Dr. Cross led us to a shed out back. He opened a large meat freezer, released the snake into the icebox, and quickly shut the lid. After the snake removal, Murray and I finished gathering wood for the night. We lit a fire in the stove, and sat at a small table playing Texas hold 'em for cigarettes. I was raking in the Marlboros, and could tell it was frustrating Murray. I too was frustrated. Murray should have taken the truck back to civilization days ago, leaving me alone with Dr. Cross, but bozo wouldn't depart.

"You boys hungry?" Dr. Cross asked.

"I'm so hungry I could eat the Lamb of God," Murray said.

"Grab three frozen pizzas from the shed," Dr. Cross said.

Inside the shed, I flipped on the light, and was about to open the lid to the icebox when I remembered the snake. I drew my gun. The rattler wasn't the only animal with a bite. I lifted the lid, and was instantly struck on the arm. I jumped back, firing my weapon into the freezer.

"I've never seen somebody so scared," Murray said, bending over and holding his side with laughter.

"What the hell?" I asked, holstering my gun, as I realized my companions stood behind me.

"You thought this guy bit you," Dr. Cross said, reaching into the freezer, pulling out the snake, and holding it before me. "It's harmless. Snakes are cold blooded, and move extremely slow when chilled."

"What got me?" I asked.

"These," Dr. Cross said, holding up his thumb and pointer finger.

"You got pinched, and shit your pants," Murray said. "Worse than a little girl."

"I'm a collector of frozen rattlesnakes," Dr. Cross said, dropping the serpent back into the freezer. "Have a look."

"Unless you're scared," Murray said.

I lit a cigarette, and glared at Murray for a moment. His insults were getting on my nerves, and I wanted him to know that it wasn't okay. After scowling at Murray, I peered inside the cooler. Amid an assortment of frozen dinners was a myriad of motionless rattlesnakes tied into various knots. I recognized the Bowline, the Clove Hitch and the Figure Eight, but there were also advanced knots I had never seen.

"Frozen snakes are pliable," Dr. Cross said, grabbing a knotted serpent, and untying it.

"Are they alive?"

"No, but they stay supple in the freezer," Dr. Cross said, retying the chilled reptile. "That is unless some goddamn idiot breaks the ice box shooting a hole in it."

He did a quick inspection of the case, and determined that I hadn't damaged the motor, coils or Freon. The Doctor said it was a good thing; otherwise, I would have joined the icy sanctuary. Murray laughed, and I gave him another sharp look, but this time he returned the favor, and we locked into a "who would blink first" pissing contest.

"Gentlemen," Dr. Cross said, breaking up the stare down, and handing me a wounded pizza box. "It's getting late."

Except for the bullet hole, that was the worst microwaved pizza I ever ate. It was lukewarm and soggy with a side of freezer burn. After dinner, we smoked cigarettes, and stoked the fire. Dr. Cross slept in the bedroom on the only bed in the cabin, so Murray and I sacked out in the living room on the floor near the stove. I tried to stay awake longer than my companion, but a profound lethargy swept over me, and I slipped into unsettling unconsciousness.

I dreamt that I was gathering wood from the pile when it collapsed on me, and dozens of rattlesnakes appeared, and wrapped themselves around my limbs in strange and complicated knots.

I woke shivering in the night, half numb from sleeping on the floor. The fire was dying. I stumbled to my feet, tripping over Murray. How was he able to snore through such Artic conditions? As I stoked the fire, I felt bad for those snakes in the cooler. Freezing was a particularly inhumane way to die. When I'm assigned a job, I try to reduce the suffering as much as possible. Two to the head usually does the job, quick and painless.

The next morning, I felt like shit. Every muscle in my body ached, my head throbbed like a strobe light of pain, and I sweated with fever.

"Wakeup," Murray said, toeing my ribs.

I stumbled dizzily to my feet, collapsing into a wooden chair at the table. I thought I was having a heart attack the way my chest hurt.

"You look sicker than Typhoid Mary," Dr. Cross said, entering from the bedroom. He handed me a white capsule. "Take this."

"What is it?"

"You'll feel better."

"But what is it?"

"Just take the damn pill," Murray barked.

As bad as I felt, I wasn't taking shit from Murray, so I flicked the pill at him. It bounced off his chest onto the floor. He picked it up, and forced the capsule between my lips. In my weakened state, I could do little to resist. I swallowed the medicine, and for a chaser, Murray slopped warm coffee on my face. Wooziness overtook me and I fell to the floor.

I woke in my darkened apartment, lying on my bed, feeling fine except for the nightmare about the little cabin in the woods. The light turned on. I wasn't home in my bed, and it wasn't a bad dream. I was still in the cabin, and Dr. Cross and Murray stood over me.

"You look better," Dr. Cross said, placing a hand on my forehead.

I climbed out of bed, naked.

"Your clothes are folded neatly on the table in the other room."

"And my piece?"

"On the table."

I pushed past Dr. Cross and Murray. I grabbed my weapon. It was still loaded. After I dressed, Dr. Cross and Murray joined me in the cabin's main room.

"How are you feeling?" The doctor asked.

"Fine," I said.

"Maybe something you ate?" Dr. Cross asked.

"Yeah," Murray said. "Maybe you have a weak stomach."

"Since you've recovered, would you fetch some wood for the stove?" Dr. Cross asked.

Outside the air was crisp and cold. I breathed deep and felt invigorated. As I cautiously gathered firewood, listening for rattlers, I decided to give Murray a chance to leave, and if he didn't take the offer, he'd also receive two to the head. I carried the wood inside and set it down by the stove. Dr. Cross and Murray ate microwaved scrambled eggs and sausage.

"I can handle things from here on out," I said to Murray. "Be on your way now."

"You can?" Murray asked after smirking and shoveling the rubbery eggs into his yap. "You've been in-and-out of consciousness for two days, talking in tongues. Think I'll stick around."

"Eat something," Dr. Cross said.

"Ain't hungry," I said, and went outside for a cigarette.

"Get more wood," Dr. Cross said as I closed the door.

I gave that chump Murray a chance to beat it. I struck a wooden match, and held it to my cigarette just as the world's longest rattlesnake slid across the yard. I drew my gun and pointed it at the serpent in pure terror, but then I remembered Dr. Cross' grotesque menagerie of frozen rattlesnakes. I didn't want this fellow ending up like those other poor bastards, so I let the limbless monster escape into the brush.

When the cigarette ended, I fingered the trigger of my pistol and resolved to put two to each head inside the cabin, fast and painless. Exactly how I liked it. One moment they would be alive, the next moment they'd be dead. I swung open the front door, and bang, bang, bang, bang.

"Missing something?" Murray said, holding the firing pin to my gun.

"No Wood?" Dr. Cross asked, chewing a breakfast sausage as Murray knocked the weapon out of my hand, and dealt me a crushing blow to the head with the stove's iron poker.

I woke with a splitting headache. My wrists and knees tied with rope. The room was dark. I had no idea where I was until Dr. Cross and Murray opened the door. I realized I was in the shed on the ground next to the freezer.

"How do you feel?" Dr. Cross asked.

"Answer the doctor," Murray said, toeing my ribs.

"Exciting news," Dr. Cross said after I didn't answer. He removed a massive rattlesnake from the freezer. "While dragging you to the shed, we spied the longest specimen I have ever seen. Truly a marvel of nature."

Dr. Cross tied the snake into a hangman's noose, and placed it around my neck.

"Looks good on you," Murray said.

"I've been micro-dosing your food with a powder I derived from neurotoxins found in rattlesnake venom. I miscalculated the level of exposure with your pizza the other night, and the hemotoxins almost destroyed your blood cells. Without the antivenin, you would have died from internal hemorrhaging. Eventually, I meant to give you a lethal dose, but not so soon. After you tried to kill us, I sped up the process, and prepared a lethal dose for your consumption," Dr. Cross said, holding out a bottle of white powder before my eyes. "This was to be your fate until this eight-footer came along. I've never seen somebody lynched by a snake rope before. Have you Murray?"

"Nope."

"Lucky us," Dr. Cross said. "And lucky you. Hanging is less painful than succumbing to the powdered venom."

"If you let me go," I said. I'll tell you who sent me."

"Never thought of you as a squealer," Murray said, lighting a cigarette. "Have a side of dignity with your death, huh."

"You were sent by our mutual employer, yes?" Dr. Cross said with a smile.

I didn't say anything as the anger welled inside me.

"Answer the doctor," Murray said, toeing my ribs.

"I asked the organization to send me a test subject for my powdered venom, and you drew the assignment."

"Dumbass," Murray said.

"Let's string him from the tree in the front yard," Dr. Cross said.

Murray grabbed the head of the frozen snake, and dragged me across the shed's floor. I gasped for air as the blood in my head pounded in my ears, and the snake noose tightened around my neck. Just before I lost consciousness, Murray yelped, and let go of the snake.

"Fucker bit me," he said, holding his wrist as the reptile around my neck loosened and untied itself.

I breathed deep, letting the oxygen fill my lungs as the snake coiled and struck Dr. Cross on the leg. The doctor cried out in pain. Murray unloaded his pistol into the serpent. The wounded viper twisted and writhed as Dr. Cross crushed its head with the sole of his boot.

"Shoot him too," Dr. Cross said, pointing at me. "I'll get the antivenin."

Murray smiled, and drew his pistol. With considerable effort I sat up against the side of the freezer. As Murray pointed the pistol at my head, I closed my eyes. The gun fired, and I fell into darkness.

Something in the distance roused me. It sounded close yet far away. A familiar popping noise that I couldn't quite place. My eyes opened, and I saw the mutilated snake, twisted and torn on the floor. My head throbbed with pain, and thirst dried my throat. Other than the head wound from the iron poker, I had no injuries. After considerable effort, I sat up against the freezer, and felt a sharp metal edge at the corner of the icebox. It took time, but I sawed off the ropes binding my wrists. My palms and fingers burned as the blood returned. After the tingling was mostly gone, I untied my knees, and gathered my equilibrium.

I opened the freezer and scraped out a piece of frost amid the knotted snakes. When the frost became liquid, I slaked my thirst. A ray of light seeped through a bullet hole in the wall. I went outside, and in the yard, I saw Dr. Cross lying on his back, covered in blood. The familiar popping sounds that had roused me in the shed had been gunshots. Murray sat against the trunk of the tree. His eyes fluttered, and foam dripped from his mouth. He mumbled something that I couldn't hear, so I drew nearer, keeping my eye on the gun in his lap.

"FBI … please … antivenin."

I disarmed Murray, and searched the cabin for the antivenin. As I tore apart Dr. Cross' room, I pieced together a scenario of the recent events that led me to this favorable outcome. The massive snake in the freezer was cold, but still alive when it was tied into a noose. It warmed against my neck and reanimated enough to bite Murray as he dragged me across the floor. The rattler then struck Dr. Cross before meeting its demise.

Murray was supposed to off me while Dr. Cross grabbed the antivenin, but Murray was an FBI agent, so he didn't shoot me. The bullet hole in the side of the shed suggested that he intentionally fired wide, and I passed out from fear of execution. While I was unconscious, Dr. Cross and Murray must have quarreled, but about what I can't say. Maybe Dr. Cross figured Murray for FBI all along, and withheld the antivenin from him. When Murray was denied the cure, and began succumbing to the snake's venom, he shot Dr. Cross, but was unable to locate the antivenin before losing control of his limbs. I couldn't be sure that this was what transpired while I lay bound and insensible on the shed's floor, but I didn't care. I was just happy to be alive.

I tore the cabin apart, but found no antivenin. I sat down at the table, looking at Murray's gun. Two to the head was more humane than suffering. I was about to kill my first FBI agent when I realized where the antivenin was. Outside, I leaned over Dr. Cross' corpse, and searched his blood-soaked pockets, removing two small plastic bottles. The first bottle contained powder, and the second bottle contained several white capsules.

Murray breathed shallow as I placed the pill in his mouth and tilted back his head. I hoped it wasn't too late. Even though he was FBI, Murray had saved me, and I wanted to return the favor. I lit a cigarette, and placed it between his lips, but he never inhaled.

I covered Murray's body with a blanket I found in the cabin before starting down the mountain in the truck. The windy dirt road would eventually lead me to my employer's place of business. Two to that bastard's head was too quick and painless of a way for that double-crosser to die. A snake slithered across the road in front of the truck. I braked and felt the bottle of powder in my pocket as the serpent slid into the brush.

Red Pop

After getting out of the program, I land a job at a convenient store. I'm required to wear a white polo shirt and khaki slacks. The attire makes me feel douchey.

Mr. Barnes owns the substance abuse rehab facility I cleaned up at. He also owns the halfway house I stay at, and he owns the Food Mart I work at.

I'm thankful to Mr. Barnes for the job, even if it is demeaning minimum wage bullshit. He helped me get clean, gave me a place to stay, and hooked me up with a job. It isn't ideal work, but it beats the hell out of the crummy things I used to do. Stocking TV dinners and 2-liter bottles of root beer trumps ripping off mom for a hit any day. At least, that's what I tell myself while price-tagging plastic soft drinks.

As I slap a 99¢ label on a 2-liter bottle of soda, the plastic jugs on the shelf next to me explode, followed by a deafening sound. The blast knocks me on my back, and covers me in fizzy red pop. A man in an orange ski mask points a shotgun at my face. Playing possum, supine in a pond of sticky crimson sugar water, I sneak a peek into my attacker's eyes: one brown, one blue. The blue eye twitches as he opens the till, alleviates the evening's earnings, and flees.

I used to shoot dope with a murderous scumbag with those same eyes named Eddy "Winky" Fisher.

When the police arrive, they put me through the standard rigmarole. Kindness and understanding aren't words I'd use to describe their questioning tactics. I tell them everything straight without mentioning Winky. They all seem to buy what I'm selling except for a corpulent, balding detective named Donaldson.

"Dope fiend Danny! Remember me?" He asks.

"Yeah."

"All cleaned up?"

"Sure."

"How's that working?"

"How's it look?"

"Pink's not your color."

"Can I go?"

"Your story's shit, and when I prove it, I'm stuffing your junky ass back in the can."

"Yeah?"

"Hear me out. Your hype-headed buddy shoots up the joint. Of course, you don't get done, just covered in pop. He gets the nightly earnings, and in a couple of hours, you're both higher than the price of groceries."

"Danny! Thank god you're alive," Mr. Barnes says, entering the Food Mart in a blue three-piece suit. "When I heard about the shooting, I feared the worst."

"I'm afraid you're being suckered Mr. Barnes," Donaldson says.

"Who's this?" Mr. Barnes asked, dabbing the sweat on his forehead with a silk handkerchief.

"Mr. Barnes meet detective Donaldson," I say.

"What do you mean Danny's suckering me?" Mr. Barnes asks.

"He and one of his druggy buddies robbed you. Right, Danny?"

"Someone almost killed him," Mr. Barnes says. "You should be finding the guy who did this, not blaming Danny."

After Mr. Barnes vouches for me, the police let me go. Mr. Barnes gives me a ten spot, and tells me to buy a new polo shirt. I get into my pickup truck, and head for the halfway house, but then I get an idea, and turn around my 4-banger.

At each hotspot, I park down the street, scoping crack houses, but there's no sign of Winky. Seeing those hops scoring brings back hard memories.

I call my stakeout quits just as Winky wanders out a rundown apartment building and climbs into a hooptie.

I follow as he crosses the tracks into the right side of town. Winky parks in front of a large white two-story house, walks to the front door, and is admitted inside. I wait, but Winky never comes out. After several hours, I get tired and leave.

On my way to the halfway house, a cop pulls me over, and stuffs me in the back of a squad car.

"Sorry about dicking you around at the Food Mart," Donaldson says from the front without turning around, the back of his fat baldhead directly in front of me. Eye contact occurs through the rear-view mirror. "But you know more than you're saying, so I had to bust your chops."

"I told you everything."

"We'll see," Donaldson says, lighting a cigarette. "A man comes into your shit shop, and tries to blow off your goddamn head."

"Yeah."

"And you know the sorry sack who done it, but you don't say nothing."

"I don't know who did it."

"Admirable, you cleaned up, Danny," Donaldson says, turning to face me. "Too bad Mr. Barnes has a bad habit of taking out life insurance policies on his clients shortly before they die."

"I never signed a life insurance policy,"

"Think I'm feeding you magical horseshit?" Donaldson asks, holding up a piece of paper. "Got a copy right here. Take a look. That's your John Hancock there and there."

Leaning forward, I see my signature scribbled several times on the page.

"Who were you following?"

"Nobody."

"Bet it was the guy tried to kill you."

"Why do you think that?"

"Because he led you straight to Mr. Barnes' house," Donaldson says as a ship sinks in my gut. "Ain't it a bitch, Danny? Signing up for death instead of life."

Dope sick, I filled out a stack of paperwork before gaining admittance into Mr. Barnes' drug rehab center. I didn't read any of it. Just signed all the dotted lines.

"Winky," I say.

"That-a-boy, Danny. Got a copy of his life insurance policy here somewhere too."

"Can I go?"

"Sure," Donaldson says, letting me out. "Hate to say I told you so."

I slide into my truck, and head downtown. Where else can I go? Certainly not back to Mr. Barnes' halfway house. I park in front of a rundown apartment complex, and crumple the ten spot in my hand.

Graveyard Grunge

Dried leaves crunch under feet as a sickle-celled moon slices through the fogbank, casting a yellowish tinge across gray tombstones.

"Can you two stop making out long enough to crack the Four Loko?" Charles asks after the three teens sprawl out on a dirty mausoleum.

"Wish you hadn't guzzled all the Natty Ice last night," Hal says after removing his pierced tongue from Mercedes' mouth, and the alcoholic energy drink from his safety pin covered backpack.

"Might still be some backwash," Charles says, tossing a nearby half-crushed Natural Ice toward Hal.

Hal feigns a swig, and draws from a vape pen before shotgunning the fumes between Mercedes' lips.

"Check it," Charles says, hopping off the sepulcher, and unzipping his leather jacket.

"Fuck yeah, Johnny Rotten," Hal says, using the flashlight on his iPhone to see the image on the t-shirt.

"Sid Vicious, dumbass" Mercedes says. "Even I know that. I got a razorblade if you want to make it look legit."

Charles cracks his Four Loko, jumps atop a thick gravestone, and tries keeping his balance while chugging the Taurine and malt liquor. When the can is empty, he belches, hurling the aluminum container against a large white tomb.

"Toss me the paint. I'm bored," Charles says. "I'm not watching you guys bone down in the graveyard again."

"Shut up," Mercedes says, lobbing the red acrylic aerosol can.

Charles catches and shakes the canister as he skanks to the large white tomb.

"That crypt wasn't here last night," Hal says, scrolling through pictures on his iPhone.

"God your dumb," Mercedes says, and kisses Hal.

Charles sprays an oval shaped anarchy sign on the tomb.

"We better dip," Hal says as the silhouette of somebody approaches through the fog.

"Huh?" Charles asks as an old woman with long white hair and a flowing white gown appears.

Droopy sunken yellow eyes swirl above a sickly leer, revealing needles for teeth. A pink earthworm-looking scar circles her neck.

"Holy. Shit," Mercedes says as the old lady holds a hatchet over her head.

Charles drops the paint can as the old woman grabs his wrist. Hissing, she swings the ax. Charles blocks the blow with his free hand, losing three fingers in the process, and spraying blood across the old lady's face.

Hal and Mercedes jump off the sepulcher, and dart down a row of gravesites as Charles' screams echo behind them. Unable to locate the cemetery gates in the fog, the lovers collapse against a tombstone near a willow tree as a loud hiss fills the air.

Yellow eyes glow in the darkness. The old woman in white, spattered in Charles' blood, appears through the mist, raising the hatchet over her head. Hal and Mercedes scream as the blade swings down.

A deafening sound thunders through the graveyard, and the splintered hatchet clatters against a nearby gravestone.

A stranger, holding a shotgun against his left shoulder, steps out of the fog. He wears faded blue jeans, and a brown shirt with green stripes. A white long-sleeved thermal under the t-shirt is pulled up to his elbows. Lengthy tangles of blonde hair obscure his face.

"Back away from the teens, spirit," he says in a deep voice, pumping the action.

The old woman hisses, lifting Hal by the neck, and ripping out his right eyeball with her razor-sharp teeth. A bloody geyser erupts from Hal's socket as a shotgun blast reverberates through the necropolis. No trace of the old woman remains except a bloodstained sheet, tangled in the branches of the nearby willow tree.

"Is she dead?" Mercedes asks, placing the palm of her hand against Hal's eye socket to slow the bleeding.

"Yes," the stranger says. "But not by my hand."

"But she's gone?"

"For now," the stranger says.

"Guys? Where are you?" Charles yells through the darkness.

"Over here," Mercedes says.

"What happened?" Charles asks, appearing out of the fog.

"This guy saved us," Mercedes says. "Charles, take off your shirt. Hal, call 911."

Mercedes cuts the Sid Vicious shirt in half with her razorblade, using a strip of fabric as a tourniquet for Charles' hand.

"Bitch got my eye," Hal says.

"Hal, I need you to call 911," Mercedes says, tying the other half of the shirt around Hal's face.

"Lost my phone."

"I found my fingers on the ground," Charles says, opening his good fist to reveal his digits. "Maybe they can reattach them. Where have I seen this dude before?"

"Sit down, Charles," Mercedes says. "You're in shock."

"I'm serious. He looks like that guy on all those shirts at Hot Topic. Didn't he die in the 90s?"

"The dude who hung himself masturbating?" Hal asks, trying to focus his one eye on the stranger.

"Not that guy. Fuck. What's his name?"

"Who cares," Mercedes says. "He saved our asses. Mister, you got a phone?"

"He's that dude from that band. I know it. People say he faked his death."

"You're mistaken," the stranger says with a chuckle, racking the gauge, as a cold breeze flutters his long blonde bangs to the side, revealing a gruesome hole where his face should be. "Just didn't want the old lady having all the fun. Especially when it comes to mall punks."

The fogbank snuffs out the yellowish light from a sickle-celled moon, and darkness envelops the gray tombstones as a thunderous chorus reverberates through the graveyard.

Red Christmas

Perry found out a hundred grand of the mob's money was lonesome in some backwater storage unit outside of town. His plan was simple: roll up on Christmas Day when nobody was around, take the cash, and bounce. Perry said it'd be like taking a present from a toddler, and I hoped so, but as I'd learned the hard way on multiple occasions, the best laid plans of rats and dogs usually go awry.

Perry punched in the code, and the electric gate opened. Mike drove the car down the rows until we located the unit we wanted. I busted the lock, and opened the rollup door. There it was, a hundred grand, stacked and sealed in plastic like a toddler's present. As the last of the money was stuffed in a bag, the first bullet hit Mike between the eyes.

Mike's mortal shell flopped onto the blacktop. I wished I could have done more than just leave him twitching on the asphalt, but there's not much you can do when somebody gets JFKed. Perry and the cash dove into the backseat as I ducked behind the dash, and mashed the gas. Lesson learned: the mob don't take off Christmas. As we approached the exit, the gunfire intensified. I rammed the car through the gate, and popped onto the highway. The windshield was fried, and one of the front tires was flat, but we were unscathed. I pulled into the ditch when the car would go no further. Perry grabbed the moneybag, and we crossed a field into thick woods.

We broke into a boarded-up cabin. I found a can of beans, and offered Perry half. He said there was no way he was eating cold beans for Christmas. I polished them off by my lonesome. After a nervous night, we left the cabin, and made our way through the wilderness. Thorns and brambles grabbed at our suits as we traversed deeper and deeper into the forest until we happened upon an old logging road.

Around a dirt bend, we found a truck. The door was unlocked, and the keys were in the ignition, so we commandeered the vehicle, and set out for civilization. The empty gun rack above the backseat led us to believe some backwater hick must have pulled over to go hunting. Perry opened the bag, and counted the money. A tape stuck out of an old cassette deck, and I pushed it in. "Lasagna" by Weird Al Yankovic played. We looked at each other with awkward expressions for a moment, and then we both started singing along to the "La Bamba" parody. It was the first time during this harrowing Christmas Day nightmare that I felt a modicum of respect for Perry. Too bad for him, the plan gone awry was righting itself, and he'd be dead within an hour.

The Road Beast

I'm driving over the hill in the fast lane in my beat-up blue pickup truck when this douchebag in a white BMW climbs up my ass. I retaliate by taking my foot off the accelerator without hitting the brake, and stay even with a silver Prius in the slow lane. The Beemer swerves back and forth behind us, honking and flashing its bright lights. I glance through my rearview mirror, and see the driver talking on his cellphone.

My pulse quickens. I'd prefer not to disturb the monster, but the metamorphosis begins. My palms sweat, my eyes go bloodshot, and the most unholy sounds erupt from deep within me. All rationale evaporates. Law and order become incomprehensible.

I stomp the gas, leaving the silver Prius in the dust. Despite putting the pedal to the floor, the tailgater remains ensconced upon my ass. He tries passing in the slow lane, so I veer to the right. He whips back into the fast lane, so I snap the wheel to the left, forcing him to slam on his brakes. He fishtails, but regains control, and angles his German sports car around my right rear tire, gunning the engine in the slow lane. This is the moment he's been waiting for. We're side by side. Our eyes meet. He smirks and flips me off.

The climb has been a series of curves, but now the path becomes a secluded straightaway at the summit. On this stretch, my shitty 4-banger won't keep up with this prick's luxury sedan. The apex is a section of road with no shoulder or guardrail. There is only a steep drop over the side of a cliff. As the BMW passes, I let out a primordial howl and jerk the wheel over, forcing the Beemer off the precipice.

I drive down the other side of the hill. My rage recedes, and I return to my cognitive self. After a few minutes, I hit gridlock. Traffic's stop and go for several miles. Ahead, I see flashing lights. It's probably an accident. When it's my turn to gawk and rubberneck at the situation, I realize CHP is ticketing the driver of the white BMW. Our eyes meet as I crawl by. Now I'm the one smirking.

Ticketed for driving like a douchebag. It' not as satisfying as how the road beast handled the situation, but it will certainly do. After I pass the traffic stop, congestion clears. The rest of my drive is peaceful until a red Mini Cooper climbs up my ass.

Marriage Counseling

I didn't love my wife Karen anymore. I liked her though. I loved my girlfriend, Julie. If lady justice (who has a great rack, I might add) weighed the feeling of like against the feeling of love, love weighed more every time.

Julie had been nagging me to leave Karen for a while now, so we could start our own life together. I kept telling her I would, but I needed to get my ducks lined up in a row first, and ducks sure as shit don't fall into line so goddamn easy.

I didn't want a divorce. I liked the equity I'd put into the house, and the money Karen and I managed to save, and the two cars in the garage, and all the modern amenities we had acquired throughout a successful twenty years of marriage. Divorce would destroy everything we had worked so hard to obtain.

I liked the hundred grand in life insurance I'd get if something unfortunate happened to Karen. That'd be some quality chicken scratch for Julie and I to start a new life with.

I was out to dinner with Julie, and she was carping me about calling it off with Karen, and I was telling her soon, and that was the truth because I'd finally hit on the perfect "accident" that would befall poor Karen. After dinner, I'd go home and draw a bath for my wife. Unfortunately, she'd fall asleep in the tub, and cha-ching, I'm in the bread with a new pie.

Julie had just finished her hors d'oeuvres when Donald walked into the restaurant and sat at a table near us. Donald was an old friend of Karen's and mine, and a huge gossip. If he saw me out to eat with another woman, it would be divorce city. I had to think fast, but it was too late. Before I could slip out unseen, Donald saw me, and came over.

"Paul," he said. "Good to see you."

"Donald."

"How's Karen?"

"Tired," I said. "Under the water ... I mean weather."

"Sorry to hear that," Donald said. "And who's this?"

"Oh, um, this is my sister, Julie," I said, and Julie's eyes turned to machineguns, mowing me down.

"Really? It's nice to meet you, Julie. I thought Paul was an only child."

"It's complicated," I said.

"I'm eating alone. Mind if I join you?" Donald asked.

That son of a bitch had me raked over the coals with a red-hot poker jammed up my ass. I had to endure the most awkwardly uncomfortable meal of all time. Donald wasn't buying the horseshit I fed him about Julie, and the further I went down the rabbit hole of lies, the more I unearthed a simple truth: in order to avoid the turnoff to divorce town, Donald would also need to meet with an untimely and accidental death.

About halfway through our meal, Julie got an "emergency phone call."

"I have to run," she said. "It was nice meeting you, Donald. Paul, I'm staying over at mom's place. Give me a call over there later. I want to have a word with you."

"Will do, sis."

"It was nice to meet you too, Julie," Donald said. "Paul, I thought your mother was dead?"

"It's complicated," I said. "What are your plans for the rest of the evening?"

"Nothing," Donald said. "I was thinking about heading home and watching a movie. Perhaps some Hitchcock shorts. You want to join me?"

"Yes," I said.

After dinner, I followed Donald to his dumpy rundown apartment. His flat was on the second floor, and it looked like a fucking shit bomb exploded in the living room. His belongings were strewn about everywhere. He offered me a beer. I popped the top and chugged.

The liquid courage should have helped me do the deed, but instead it had the opposite effect. I looked around, feeling sorry for Donald. He was a pathetic, lonely and dirty bachelor, but then I thought about divorce, and losing my ass. I grabbed the toaster, snuck up behind Donald as he put a copied VHS tape into the VCR, and strangled him with the chord. This was by no means an easy feat. It took a lot of time and energy to throttle Donald. He thrashed around quite a bit, and even managed to scratch my face.

The noise must have ticked off Donald's downstairs' neighbor. No sooner had I choked dead that gossipy no-good bastard, when the door burst open, and a woman in a bathrobe and curlers stood before me screaming bloody murder at the top of her lungs. It took her a few moments to stop bawling me out, and comprehend the scene before her.

"This isn't what it looks like," I said, but she wasn't having any of it, and ran screaming back to her apartment.

I gave chase, and was able to force my way into her abode before she locked the door. She was hysterical, and I needed to shut her up quick before she drew more unwanted and unnecessary attention to my surreptitious activities.

On a counter next to the door, a marble vase held a plastic flower of some sort. I couldn't tell you what kind of flower it was because I don't really know much about those sorts of things, but the vase was heavy and durable, so I picked it up, and conked her on the head with it. She went down like a sack of bricks, but gave a little moan, so I gave her a few more solid whacks with the urn until she fell silent and her face became blood pudding.

Unfortunately, her gore had splattered all over me. I went into the bathroom to wash up before making my exit, and that's when I saw a young boy of about ten, hiding in the shower stall. He was on the phone with the police. Needless to say, I was furious with the little tyke. I snatched the phone from him, told the police I was his parent, and that he was making a prank call, and then I hung up.

I just needed there to be no more witnesses, and I wouldn't have to keep killing. Why was that such a hard thing to have happen? I didn't want to finish off the kid, but goddamn it, I didn't want a divorce either, so I lifted up the toilet seat, dunked the boy's head in the pot, and sent him to his watery grave. Again, I was surprised at how hard it was to drown somebody. It took way too long, and I ended up soaked in toilet water, which was disgusting.

I grabbed a towel, and wiped away the blood and water as best I could.

As I was about to leave, a cop entered the apartment.

"Freeze," he yelled with his gun drawn. "Get your hands up."

"Thank god you're here," I said, and walked toward him. "I just got home, and found my wife, my beautiful wife, bleeding on the ground."

I tried to think about what it would be like if I had come home and found my wife dead, and it made me really sad, and I even shed a few tears. I got down on my knees, hugged the cop's leg, and started sobbing.

"Did you check for a pulse," the cop said, buying my boloney, and holstering his firearm.

As soon as he put his gun away, I grabbed it, and shot him in the head. Again, and I know I'm beating a dead horse here, I was amazed at how disturbingly gruesome a gunshot wound to the head is. The cop spasmed and twitched something awful, and I think he shit his pants.

"Finally," I thought as I made a hasty exit. "No more witnesses."

On the drive home, I couldn't stop thinking about how Julie had behaved at dinner. She was sort of being a bitch. Was that what it was going to be like with her? If that was the case, forget it.

I arrived home. Karen was already asleep. I took off all of my clothes, and burned them in the fireplace. I crawled into bed and cuddled up against Karen. What a fool I had been. I didn't like my wife. I loved her.

Previous Publication Credits

"A Hell of a Hideout," first published at *Yellow Mama*

"Arson on the Eastside," first published at *Tough*

"Burning Snow," first published in *Switchblade Magazine*

"All That Nighttime," first published at *Pulp Metal Magazine*

"Red Rocks," first published at *Tough*

"Eddie Spaghetti," first published at *Near to the Knuckle*

"The River Never Tells," first published at *Yellow Mama*

"Flower Man," first published at *Punk Noir Magazine*

"The Exterminator," unpublished story

"Charlie Knuckles," unpublished story

"Don't Be Next," first published at *Story and Grit*

"Boundaries," first published at *Ugly Dad*

"Dead Meat," first published at *Yellow Mama*

"The Con After the Storm," first published at *Near to the Knuckle*

"Sour Sixteen," first published at Out of the Gutter

"Bad Batch," first published at *Spelk*

"Finder's Fee," first published at *Shotgun Honey*

"The Turkey," first published at *Out of the Gutter*

"The Rex," first published at *Punk Noir Magazine*

"Snaked," first published at *Fried Chicken and Coffee*

"Red Pop," first published at *Out of the Gutter*

"Red Christmas," first published at *Yellow Mama*

"Graveyard Grunge," first published at *Out of the Gutter*

"The Road Beast," first published at *Flash Fiction Magazine*

"Marriage Counseling," first published at *Near to the Knuckle*

Acknowledgements

Many thanks to those who helped untangled these yarns in one capacity or another.

Big thanks to Paty Stevens, William Shakespeare, Marie Hoffman, Tom Pitts, Sole Anatrone, Jack Bates, Cindy Rosmus, Rusty Barnes, Hector Duarte, Jr., Travis Richardson, Hermann Hesse, Rob Pierce, Paul D. Brazill, Jesse Heels Rawlins, Jim Shaffer, Jason Beech, Bill Baber, Joe Clifford, Davenzane Hayes, Robert Ragan, Chris DeWildt, Mark Westmoreland, Cal Marcius, Ron Earl Phillips, Scotch Rutherford, Eric Beetner, Criag Douglas, Oliver Brennan, Patrick Whitehurst, Dietrich Kalteis, Mick Rose, Luc Alex Raphael, and the music of Paolo Conte.

About the Author

Morgan Boyd is an educator, living on the Monterey Peninsula with his wife and daughter. He has an MA in Television, Film, Radio, and Theatre from San Jose State University. Morgan has had his stories published in *Out of the Gutter*, *Switchblade Magazine*, *Near to the Knuckle*, *Yellow Mama*, *Tough*, *Punk Noir Magazine*, *Shotgun Honey*, and various other crime fiction websites. He also enjoys outdoor activities, growing chili peppers in the garden, and watching the chickens run around the yard. Morgan is currently writing a novella about a criminal in love.